"BE THE COACH OF YOUR MIND"

R. Barbero

Reinaldo Barbero

"Every change is contradictory; there-
fore, the contradiction is the true es-
sence of reality"

HERACLITUS

DEDICATION

This book is dedicated to Luis and Omaira, my parents; they taught me the art of being in the world with the best intentions, with inexhaustible curiosity and love of reading.

To Isabel, Alessandro and Clarissa, my beloved wife and my beloved children, the strength of love that can do everything, in times of peace, and in turbulent times.

Jorge and Francisca, my second parents, the best example of dedication to the cause of man always possible.

My dear brothers, the biological ones and the gifts of life.

To everyone who loves the effort to be better.

TABLE OF CONTENTS

I.

Foreword.

Greetings dear reader. I invite you, in the next pages of this book, to delve into the hidden spaces of the mind, and open a wide area to the powerful capacity for self-analysis, reflection and imagination that this governing body of our actions offers us; the *brain*.

As you will surely know, there reside the nuclei that shape our personality, as a consequence of a long process of adaptations that begin as soon as we see the light of this world. We can say with total certainty, that in this wonderful organ, we store the early experiences, which helped to form a differentiated person, a character differentiated from the rest that makes us unique and unrepeatable. I advance you that in order to take on the challenge of this book being a guide, to start a personal journey, it is mandatory that we divide the task into parts. You see, it is not easy, but not impossible, to access long-held content stored in our *mind*, or what we call in Psychology "psyche", from the Latin. These primitive contents, which were indelibly shaped in areas of our brain, give shape to the configuration of a *mind*, a particular and *idiosyncratic*[1] psychism, in a network of attitudes, dispositions, preferences, tastes, and ultimately, particular behaviors. Now, for the purposes of this journey that we started, we are going to detail what behavior is, because as you can already guess, it is the visible part of our psyche. We cannot guess the thoughts, decipher preferences and tastes and motivations in a simple way, only through careful observation of behavior or attitudes, we will begin to develop the ability and competence to understand more strongly and without fear of being wrong, that it pushes the behavior, what is behind, that motivates a particular way of being. Likewise and based on these keys, we will learn to decipher ourselves, to understand ourselves and, in sum, to deliver our maximum potential, knowing that it is a laudable goal and perhaps one of our greatest desires, to be ourselves, free of emotional commitments and psychological that dominate our actions, that subject our freedom, the true internal freedom, which takes us to the peak of our development; without limitations, without imposed barriers; full personal development in total harmony with the world. We will only understand this, if we commit ourselves to devote time and effort to understand the mechanism of the psyche, how the mind can master us, or on the contrary, how we can master and put at the service of our illusions, our brain potential. If you take on the challenge, I invite you to go ahead and continue reading. Please take note and use this manuscript as a travel journal, with which you can reflect on how you have been performing, as you have been delivering your best performance, or on the contrary, what you need to take a step forward, which requires to be best. I warn you that it will not be easy, that you may have the tendency to stop reading, to stop thinking, to deviate from the goal, to give in to the effort of looking inward, of paying the tributes of personal growth. But that is already foreseen, it is already known that on this trip, we will make short or long stops and on occasion, we will like to return to the beginning, because self-analysis will push us into a territory where we will not be the same person. If you assume the challenge with fullness and confidence, you will necessarily be moving towards an improved version of your human person. There lies the goal of this effort, it has objectives and it will know on its own, without help from anyone, how much progress was made in that path, or what tasks are still pending. That final balance will be at your disposal and you will decide what to do eventually, without anything or anyone conditioning you. This book is at the philosophical and ideological antipodes, of formulas according to which it must assume preconceived attitudes that are alien to it, that alienate and stun it to see itself, and be the owner of its emotional wellbeing to be free, once and for all. Successes!

R. Barbero, Maracaibo, Enero de 2019.

II.

About the mind, the brain and its laws.

That wonderful and sophisticated organ conformed by an unspeakable number of nerve cells called neurons, of different types, has separated us in the evolutionary scale of the animal kingdom, and has given us the supremacy, to dominate this world over the rest of the species.

In the embryological development, Homo sapiens, acquires a superior value when structured at the cellular level, in a highly specialized biological organism and with a neural cord dominated by a wide and complex cortex, whose form and capacity, gives the pattern for thought forms complex, develop the language and superior executive functions that define us as a species. But we know that it was not always like that; H. Sapiens Sapiens is the result of a long phylogenetic process in a journey of millions of years, which passed through more primary phases (*Australopithecus Afarensis, Neanderthal, Homo habilis up to Homo Sapiens Sapiens*), which resulted in what we are today . It is not the objective of this manuscript to assume any dogmatic position on how all of the above happened, simply for now we are interested in describing the basic aspects of our evolution as a biological organism. Because of this, and due to the cellular complexity described, we were able to develop processes within the cerebral cortex, increasingly complex and articulated to specific functions. Thus, the symbolic capacity to communicate, went from simple but aesthetic cave paintings, on the walls and roofs of the caves that gave us shelter, to alphabets with their own morphology, adapted to the geographical areas of the planet Earth. This symbolic capacity triggered increasingly elaborate thought processes, based on language, on its fundamental structure (morphological conformation that gives meaning to various syntaxes), to frame the field of human action, so that through language, we delimit the behaviors, by naming and meaning the whole panorama of possible behaviors and actions.

The categories were born: *good - bad, accepted - forbidden, peace - war, friend - enemy, healthy - poisonous*, etc., in alphabets with their own rules to name these events and circumstances of human daily life. All in the most basic levels of communication (non-verbal), even the most elaborate (complex writing). The Sumerians already gave guidelines on how to gather symbols full of meaning, to articulate a form of *cuneiform* writing that is known to be the origin of many later written forms. We arrived in that long journey, to modern man, with a broad cerebral cortex (maximum capacity in cubic centimeters inside the cranial vault, having a corrugated design with convolutions and fissures), with the rudiments of a complex oral and written communication system and grouped into increasingly dynamic clans, tribes and villages. Above all, H. Sapiens developed complex mental processes, which led him to project his imaginative capacity beyond his body, articulating rituals destined to worship the telluric forces of the planet. He carved figures to which he attributed powers over nature, carved stones of all sizes to delimit ritual spaces and astronomical functions, and began to worship those figures that represented diverse powers: air, earth, water and fire. The power of the wind, the power of rain, the power of the earth and the mystery of lake and ocean waters.

Little by little, its gregarious conformation gave way to nomadic communities that later saw the need to settle in a geographical space, and since then, attachments to the land and geography were generated, gave way to the concept of town, territory, kingdom and country. Characteristic symbols of these conglomerates were assumed, and a territorial identity was generated that delimited borders and set limits, proliferating kingdoms and kings, towns and manors, initiating a hierarchical scale that became a form of domination of some over others. But not only the will, motivation and individual effort for the right to territory and its resources began to be dominated; The hegemony of ideas, concepts, cults and rituals was also established to exert control over the masses of people.

It is the history of humanity. Why? We'll see later. Innate impulses in H. Sapiens. Instincts of survival. Power fight. Longing for control. In short, an explosive mixture of instinctive urgencies, which have become a long list of catastrophes, largely halting the progress of human consciousness towards more humanistic stages.

But let us focus our attention on the psychological dimension of man. Up to now we have a panorama of a bio-genetic and socio-historical progression, that has made a human society like the one we have today, but *can man progress in his human development in the middle of this complex scenario? Is the maximum development of the person still viable under these circumstances? Is it possible to acquire a higher level of awareness about our capabilities and potentials in the midst of the planetary crisis?* The answer has to be positive. Yes you can take a step in the ascending step of development, only as we said before, is a sine qua non requirement, stop to analyze your own psyche, your own mind, your own achievements and results until the present moment. With a retrospective view of our life, we can project credible changes in the future tense.

An exhaustive review of my achievements, failures, shortcomings, mistakes, oversights and accumulated forgetfulness, give me clues as to where I should begin the path of personal change. This process, apparently obeys an innate condition of man, which pushes him to seek personal and societal improvement. Let's detail the process of the mind.

According to Ferrater Mora (2000), as an entity, the concept of mind[2], already represented a debate in classical Greece; Are the mind of the body separate substances? Do they interact with each other? Are they ultimately reducible to just one? In the classical dualist tradition of Plato, they are separate entities; but for the interactionism of Descartes, both interact in the pineal gland. In *structuralism*[3], they are entities that have parallel influences, because they run in parallel currents, so that what impacts the mind, impacts parallel to the body in a term of *psychophysical parallelism*[4]. In the field of Gestalt psychology, there is an *isomorphism*[5] between mind and body, so that there is a point-by-point correspondence between the conscious experience and the physical situation, but not in an identical way. It can be said that it is like a map, where the external reality is interpreted but it is not necessarily similar, nor a faithful copy of the world.

In the behavioral psychological system, the individual is studied, their responses and their mental processes, without much attention to the ultimate nature of the *mind-body relationship*. But let's go back to the concept or idea of what the mind is. In the tradition of psychological science, it can be conceptualized as the organized totality of all psychological processes, which allow the individual to interact with their surrounding environment. From a structuralistic point of view, it is the totality of conscious experiences.

But it is still not entirely clear: what is the *mind*? Let us continue to deepen in the light of the opinions of *phenomenological* experts such as Valera, Thompson and Rosch (1997), who have contributed an integrating vision between Western science and Buddhist philosophy, about what is considered *mind* and *consciousness*, and the psychological product called I:

> *Following Descartes, "... the mind in the Western philosophical tradition is a subjective consciousness that contains ideas that correspond (or fail to correspond) with what was in the world. They refer these authors, that this vision of a mind that represented the world, reached its culmination in the notion of intentionality of Franz Brentano[6]. According to Brentano, all mental states (perception, memory, etc., are of or about something, in their words, mental states have by force "reference to their content" or "direction to an object" (which is not necessarily one thing in the world.) This direction or intentionality, according to Brentano, was the defining characteristic of the mind. (This intentional use should not be confused with the meaning of "doing something with purpose.") E. Husserl[7] was a student of Brentano and continuing his work In one of his main works, Ideas: general introduction to a pure phenomenology published in 1913, Husserl tried to develop a specific procedure to examine the structure of intentionality, which was the structure of experience itself, without any reference to the factual, empirical world, he called this procedure "put in parentheses" (epoché), since it required putting apart, as in parentheses, the vulgar judgments about the relationship between experience and the world. He called "natural attitude" the point of view from which these vulgar judgments are made; it is the attitude generally called "naive realism", which consists in the conviction that the*

world is independent of the mind or cognition and that things are generally as they appear. By bracketing the thesis of the natural attitude, Husserl argued that he could study the intentional contents of the purely internal mind, that is, without following the trace to its apparent reference in the world. Through this procedure, he claimed to have discovered a new domain that was prior to all empirical[8] science. Husserl tried to reduce the experience to these essential structures and then show how our world is generated from them. Husserl thus took the first step of the reflective scientist by arguing that to understand cognition we cannot take the world naively, but we must see that the world bears the mark of our own structure. He also took the second step, at least partially, by noting that this structure (the first step) was something he was knowing by his own mind. In the philosophical modality of its western tradition, however, it did not take the steps discussed before. He began with a solitary individual conscience, understood that the structure he was looking for was purely mental and accessible to the conscience in an act of abstract philosophical introspection, and from there he had great difficulties to general the consensual and intersubjective world of human experience. And having no other method than his own philosophical introspection, he certainly could not make the final maneuver to return to his experience, the beginning of the process. The irony of the Husserlian procedure, then, is that Husserl claimed to be directing philosophy towards a direct confrontation with experience but ignored the consensual aspect and the direct corporeal aspect of the experience. F. Valera, Thompson and Rosch (1997), continuing clarifying that the pure phenomenology of Husserl as a method, lacking a pragmatic and less theoretical dimension to understand the world of ideas, led to an existentialist phenomenology, at the hand of Merleau-Ponty, who highlighted, like Heidegger, the pragmatic and corporeal context of human experience, but in a purely theoretical way, although one of Heidegger's main arguments against Husserl was the impossibility of separating the lived experience of the Consensual Background from cultural beliefs and practices - apart from the fact that in a Heiddegerian analysis one cannot, strictly speaking, speak of a Human mind apart from that Background - even Heidegger considered phenomenology as the true method of ontology, a theoretical inquiry into human existence (Dasein) that was logically prior to any form of scientific inquiry. Merleau-Ponty[9] took Heiddegger a step further by applying Heidegger's critique to phenomenology itself, as well as to science. According to Merleau-Ponty, both science and phenomenology explained our concrete and corporeal existence so that it was always post factum. He tried to apprehend the immediacy of our non-reflexive experience and tried to give him a voice in conscious reflection. But precisely because it was a theoretical activity post factum could not capture wealth of experience. Merleau-Ponty admitted it in his own way, saying that his task was infinite. Within our Western tradition, phenomenology was and is the philosophy of human experience, the only building of thought that addresses these issues bluntly. But, first of all, it was and is philosophy as theoretical reflection. In most of the Western tradition since the Greeks, philosophy is the discipline that seeks to find the truth, including the truth about the mind, in pure form, through abstract and theoretical reasoning. Even philosophers who criticize or problematize reason do so only through argumentations, demonstrations and - especially in this so-called postmodern age - linguistic exhibitions, that is, through abstract thought. The critique of science and phenomenology undertaken by Merleau-Ponty, saying that they are post-factum theoretical activities, can equally be applied to most of Western philosophy as theoretical reflection. In this way, the loss of faith in reason, rampant in much of current thinking, simultaneously transforms into a loss of faith in philosophy.

But if we move away from reason, if reason is no longer taken as a method to know the mind, what to turn to? One possibility is unreason and, probably, through psychoanalytic theory, has reached greater influence on our popular western conception of the mind than any other cultural factor.

Very well; until now we see how in the western scientific tradition, efforts have been made to understand how the mind interprets the external reality. We saw that it is not a simple process, to separate the mechanisms by which the mind apprehends the world, but these efforts have continued and it is necessary that we review them with the most current perspectives, in order to understand how the mind and its Products (ideas, thoughts, feelings, memories, imagination, creativity, planning, etc.) give meaning to our relationship with the world. This is key to continue with the purpose of this book, which seeks to provide some clues about how we can recognize mental processes, which are harmful and hindering us to progress in life. Continuous failures, failed attempts, recurrent forgetting, mental blocks; that impede our progress and that we do not know that they occur in the background of our mind, putting the brakes on the deployment of our maximum intellectual and human potential. But we have to leave the Phenomenology and its methods to enter the field of *Cognitive Sciences*, which by recognizing the methods of the oriental (non-western) Buddhist philosophies of India, China, Korea, Japan and Tibet; they have accommodated a range of ways to increase full consciousness or *mindfulness*[10], by making present the corporeal experience, which makes us experience a reality in a more present way in the mind; also known in the West as *awareness*[11] or open consciousness. In this regard, let's see the works advanced by Dr. Jhon Kabat-Zinn:

"... Dr. Jhon Kabat-Zinn, a US doctor, has been developing research since 1979 focused on mind-body interactions for health and the clinical applications of mindfulness meditation training for people with chronic pain and problems or stress-related disorders, including studies of the effects of the REBAP technique on the brain and how it processes emotions, especially under stress. Kabat-Zinn has carried out scientific trials to test the effects of the REBAP technique (stress-based reduction of mindfulness) on the brain in different populations potentially subjected to stress: in prison inmates and their staff, in multicultural environments and in work environments He has also published studies on the effect of mindfulness on the immune system, for example, rates of reduction of skin lesions in patients with psoriasis and rejection rates in recipients of bone marrow transplants. These last works suffer from low methodological quality: the sample is low and, in addition, either there is no blinding or this is partial ...".[12]

We can then friend reader, begin to better understand how the psychological process that occurs within us and we call mind, which has tried to be explained from ancient philosophical traditions and then by diverse scientific approaches, is a *psychophysical phenomenon* that from the ancient Greeks, going through the Buddhist traditions of meditation and full consciousness, and even European phenomenological techniques; mediates human experience with its surrounding environment and within the self, and when it is focused internally with intensity, in the state that is called meditation, it can be focused on a single object that can generate a state of relaxation that is beneficial to both psychological and medically conditions. It can also be a *dissociated state* where trance can be given, and it can also be a mystical state, where superior realities or religious objects are experienced, according to Varela, Thompson & Rosch (1997). With all this, you will have already noticed that there are tangible benefits that provide reflection, meditation and relaxation when they are launched intentionally and with a therapeutic objective, so it is a practice that is highly recommended to incorporate our usual repertoire of healthy activities. As we will see later, and advancing in the domain of the method called *coaching*[13], these principles are fundamental for us to reach a necessary degree of freedom, which cuts the dogmatic ties that mediate our ability to be fully aware of our current experience. It is an objective of this book, to carry the message of healthy independence, the full freedom to decide consciously, what actions and steps we must take to progress as individuals, with temporary support when the possibilities are exhausted, but once aware of our potential, start the journey towards *self-realization* as the most expensive humanistic goal. Always avoiding the Barnum Effect[14], according to which we have the tendency to believe as valid the oracles and forecasts of third parties. Only with full awareness of our mental processes, their impact and importance in our psychological world and in the social environment, we can direct and master them to put them at the service of our progress. That is the aspiration of this book that can contribute to the reflection of personal and human improvement.

Now, if we look closely, the *"conscious"* word has been repeated and it may be asked, is there perhaps an *unconscious* experience that my mind also knows? Effectively. Here we have to clarify that those psychological processes that make up the mind, happen at various *levels of consciousness*. But, how is that of *consciousness* and *mind*? We will see that they are related but different processes. My mind produces images at a level that I cannot consciously perceive (for example during sleep) and those images if we remember them once awake, impact the field of our consciousness. The *levels of consciousness* can be: *sleep, wakefulness, coma* and other *altered states* (*hypnosis, trance induced by psychoactive substances, shamanic trance*, among others).

These states are *electroencephalographically* (which can be measured by the bioelectric potential of the brain) different from each other, presenting different patterns and cycles (hertz per second). While reading this manuscript, your *consciousness* is in the electroencephalographic state of "vigil", and when you go to bed to sleep, your brain will move from the waking state to the sleep state, going through a brief *transient* state prior to the change of electroencephalographic pattern, proper to the dream (change of cerebral cycling or wave type), and you will be peacefully asleep until you wake up, which reverses the process; in this case from sleep to wakefulness.

With a varied vision of the concept of mind and its states of consciousness, but clear at the point that they are psychological processes that occur within the individual (in the brain predominantly), we can practice some reflections or meditations, to begin to warm the muscle of auto analysis and exercise innate abilities, which only require our attention to be activated in the service of our development if we so decide. With some practical exercises, we will begin to have contact with this internal reality and its possibilities. Let's use a classic exercise to enhance *mindfulness*, and *awareness* or open awareness. For them, it is a requirement to "calm my body", to capture what my conscience (my mind) processes, and to realize its contents. Then you will have to work with those contents (which is the goal of *self-applied coaching*), but for now let's practice this:

In a comfortable position, sitting or lying down, after taking three deep breaths, ask yourself the following question:

What can I capture in my mind at this time?

Now try to "capture" everything that you see projected into your consciousness or your conscious mind at that moment. Everything that goes through it, including *sensations* and *emotions*. It can be an *image*, a *physical sensation*, a *feeling* or an *emotion*, an *imperative* or *compulsive desire*, a *persistent memory*. Whatever appears in your consciousness, is what predominates. Very well, now to start the process of full consciousness, we must apply the opposite, that is, removing the attention from the mental process, and focus on the body, for example in the breath, its rhythm and periodicity. As the air enters, as it passes through the nose, through the respiratory tract, as it enters our lungs and then as it exit in the expiration. Attentive to that rhythmic cycle, the come and go. What sensations does it generate? This process removes attention in the sometimes automatic and uncontrolled flow of thought, and focuses the mind towards the body, quieting it in its functioning and opening the space to a new consciousness, more quiet and focused in the internal.

This is how the exercise is intended, it only intends that you look inward at your mental-psychological process, and that you learn to capture the contents of the consciousness at a certain moment, and how you can reverse the attention to the body, by reversing the preponderance or supremacy of one process over the other. Very well, we already know that there are differences between what we know as mind, consciousness, levels of consciousness and thought. We have briefly learned to capture our thoughts and sensations that appear, almost automatically, in our mind at a specific time and can be sometimes annoying or persistent, or can be motivating and enjoyable (activating full awareness and open awareness - mindfulness and awareness). Thus, as we have been saying, in the space we call mind, there is the complex *thought*[15] process, which when it has an altered course and an unreal content, produces a *dissociation*[16] of the surrounding reality and causes mental illness.

The healthy functioning of the mind and especially the thought process produces ideas that are adjusted to the world, creative, pragmatic, useful and beneficial for the person and their environment. A mental disorder (psychological or psychiatric), which produces delusional ideas (for example *nihilists*[17] ideas), is indicative of a serious problem of adjustment to the internal world and the surrounding environment, generating a complex pathological entity that disintegrates the personality and all its components (character, habits, cognitive performance, memory, identity, spatial location in time and place, etc.). The conscious and voluntary exercise to focus your resources on superior processes through *immediate and corporeal experience*[18], will help you to dismantle harmful habits that have solidified as personal beliefs and fantasies that as particular and varied *complexes*[19] (inferiority or superiority, idealization, fiction and fantasies, etc.), generate maladaptive behavior and self-sabotage. This tour, as you will see later on, as you progress in reading and practice, if you decide; it will generate a positive *crisis identity*[20], in the sense that it will remove your way of seeing the world that will lead you to have higher levels of adjustment and integration to the social environment, showing your best human version. Now let's review how the mind, by means of intelligence, represents the world in different ways. This concept is key in *Cognitivism*[21] in assuming that the mind (the thinking subject) represents in its cerebral system, relevant features of the situation in which it is found and to the extent that this representation of the situation is accurate, the behavior of the agent will succeed (Varela, Thompson & Rosch, 1997). It is not easy to understand the representational mechanism that produces behaviors, because for neurosciences, it is a requirement to demonstrate methodologically, where those representational processes occur at the cellular (cerebral) level. However, it is known that representation has its symbolic component that is grouped into *semantic*[22] relationships that give meaning, through syntactic rules, to thought and its products (words, sentences, speeches, arguments, interpretations, etc.).

Cognitive science and *neuroscience,* has not yet been able to reduce to its minimum element the thought process in its physical correlate (tangible elements within the brain) to fully understand how symbols are articulated under semantic and syntactic rules that generate cognitions (thought) and language. *Artificial intelligence* (AI)[23] tries to imitate human cognitive functions such as learning that lead machines to solve complex problems. But this is just a computational exercise based on mathematical formulations that have a limit on the probabilities of courses of action that occur in human relationships, so for now; its possibilities are limited to complex processes and tasks and for specific purposes, and at no time it emulates the very high variability of human behavior. Under semantic and syntactic rules, scientists can give life to machines to emulate some human behaviors, but it has not yet been possible to replicate experimentally the human mind and its deep and complex processes, being a scientific aspiration as a frontier to be explored over the years to come.

As stated by Varela, Thompson and Rosh (1997), *"... but the basic idea that the brain is a device to process information that reacts to certain environmental characteristics persists at the core of modern neuroscience and public perception ...".*

Up to this point, we have made a low flight through the history of the concept of mind; to know how the psyche intercedes in our behavior and attitudes; let us now turn to the domain of Psychology as a positive science that laid the foundations for the detailed analysis of behavior, its causes and consequences. First from Psychoanalysis as a psychological science of the deep mind and introduce a new paradigm about the structure of the mind: *conscious*[24], *preconscious* and *unconscious*[25]; until the Behaviorism (that focused its object in the behavior like unit of primary analysis). For psychoanalysis, the cognitive thesis was fundamental, in the sense of attributing to the mental thought process (*ideas, images, dreams, memories, language,* etc.) a particular *intentionality*[26]. He searched the ideas as a reflection of the instincts to isolate the variable with impact on mental health. He came to postulate a deeper level of the mind, which he called the unconscious with the ability to dominate behavior through psychic and behavioral acts charged with affectivity (of any tone) but subordinated to the primary instincts of survival, reproduction and aggression.

Now, this means that the contents of the mind, are highly intervened by the unconscious level, which has its own dynamics and can push (motivate) the behavior to pro social or sociopathic goals. Here we enter a quite complex territory, which proposes that in order to reach the desired state of optimum mental health, it is necessary to make conscious, those contents (*repressed*) that are pressing to capture our attention with acts beyond our comprehension. This state of maximum psychic stability, will be reached if and only yes, we devote time and effort in elucidating those contents loaded with *affective power*, to be able to take them to the field of conscious and detailed analysis that they discover once and for all, their true motivations and hidden needs. For the purposes of this book, this journey will have to be done through the intentional reflection on our behaviors, failed acts, omissions and errors of appreciation and relationship, which have placed us in the current stage of personal development. We are what we are until now, but we can try an analysis of our underlying behaviors and roots, to be able to clarify what is pushing my events and how I can in a determined way, change to improve as a person, couple, father or mother, friend, citizen, worker, supervisor; anyway; be a better human being. This process, we will try in the second chapter.

Let's see now how *Behavioral Psychology*[27] as a discipline of the study of the mind, went on to focus its analysis method away from the phenomenological field (introspection and meditation), to rely on tangible systems of measurement of acts, as a basic unit of behavior and as objective reality, observable and instrumentally measurable.

Then left the behavioral psychologists, to use the mental image as an element of analysis and turned to the measurement of behaviors, as programmable units through universal and fundamental laws of human and animal learning: *positive and negative reinforcement, positive and negative punishment , extinction, classical conditioning, operant conditioning*, etc. Using quantitative methods, he was able to quantify the magnitudes of the behaviors to redirect them and produce observable and lasting behavioral changes. *Behavioral Therapy*[28] and *Applied behavioral analysis*[29] (ABA under the premises of *Operant Conditioning*[30]), contribute greatly to moderate disruptive behaviors in children with various types of disorders (*autism spectrum disorders or ASD*, *developmental disorders and adaptive disorders of diverse type, etc.*), and it is a great advance for the field of Psychology, as a positive science at the service of the improvement of human capacities. Likewise, by applying specific and intentional *reinforcements* at the opportune and foreseen time, the probabilities of establishing (learning), behaviors permanently in the *behavioral repertoire*, are greatly increased, according to the Clinical child psychologist Isabel Montiel (2019). This specialist proposes that this technique, applying it with persistence and discipline, achieves amazing results which she summarizes with a phrase recommended by her political mother, *"Do not lower your guard"*.

In this book, we will find clues to analyze our own behavior by becoming sharp observers of behaviors that we can modify, if we propose it. Only by becoming aware of how behaviors of different types and purposes are installed and learned can we be able to isolate and reinforce them or eliminate them from our range of options. That is a challenge that I invite you to assume if you continue going into the pages of this journey through your psyche.

As we have already seen, philosophy and psychology as rigorous and universal disciplines can be very helpful in understanding the *epiphenomenon*[31] called *mind*, psyche, originated (and we do not extend ourselves in the phenomenon of consciousness and its possible non-locality) in the brain. In this body, as we already mentioned, there are structures, nuclei and networks with specific functions. For example, the so-called *Broca area*[32] is the center associated with the language; the *amygdala*[33], which as part of the so-called *limbic system*[34], is responsible for emotional regulation, which, incidentally, is only found in higher mammals.

Thus, we discover the complexity of these structures and nuclei, which ultimately predispose us innately, to behave as human beings. Pathologies in specific areas, generate specific mental syndromes as expected: mood disorders and affectivity (*bipolarity*[35], depression, and mania), personality disorder, *schizophrenia*[36], etc. The latter is a quite serious and complex syndrome, which has as a main symptom among others, the *depersonalization*[37] or loss of personality of the sufferer. It is terrible when the person looks in the mirror and no longer recognizes himself as him or her. I cease to exist that person. All this happens in the brain and in the mental sphere, so we have to have a basic knowledge of how these mechanisms work, if we want to get into this interesting field with the appropriate tools. Here we will touch some aspects of the mind that can play tricks or confuse us in our appraisals, because they represent another type of mental activities such as those described, and that escape from the will of change of the person, that is, before a serious mental disorder, what which prescribes is urgent psychiatric help. From the medical model, these disorders can be treated with different degrees of success and *prognosis*[38].

Doing a review up here, you can appreciate a reader, to continue with a firm base, in the analysis and application of *self-help* tools and personal and professional development such as *coaching* (so fashionable today), is a must, to be informed of which underlying processes and mechanisms move human behavior.

There are principles, there are laws that are universally proven (for example, human and animal learning experimentally verified in the laboratory), they are the frame of reference of *neuro-*

sciences and *behavioral sciences*, to describe and prescribe, formulas of change with certain bases (remember that behavioral models of behavior modification have: high degree of structuring of their procedures, systematic evaluation of progress in treatment or training, use of modeling and chaining by simplifying in simpler units, complex behaviors, differential reinforcement of incompatible behaviors with which it seeks to eliminate, among many other quantifiable methods). We can put *faith*[39] in the recipes and recommendations, and that is a factor of importance that we will see later to overcome many types of personal crises; but to get to the conviction about how the mind works and how it affects us, we need concrete data, concrete methods of approach, measurable scientific knowledge on how and to what degree or level changes the behavior, changes the person and improves their human performance , to be able to apply them to ourselves with confidence and certain base. We can move forward and we can help others on that trip.

In the next chapter, we will focus on *coaching*, its methods and its importance in the *digital age*[40], and how we can apply those principles (already with a minimum knowledge base) to start the path of personal development as humans and start being more free and independent. Let's keep going.

III.

Coaching, its methods and Globalization 4.0

Talking about *coaching*[41] is talking about many forms of guidance and tutoring. Let's start by clarifying how the term is born, and how it was applied to various ways and activities of accompaniment, which resulted in a particular *epistemology*[42] of the counseling process, for personal and professional improvement. We will step on an ambiguous terrain in its origins, but that after clarifying fundamental historical aspects, it will open the door to the domain of the helping profession in which it has been transformed. This is important, given that we are not considering a new concept and practice, on the contrary, a role played by people trained and dedicated to this altruistic work was based on these ancient practices.

According to L. Ravier (2005), coaching has varied origins, however it clarifies how and why it appears associated with the word coach, let's see:

"... The story goes back to the 15th and 16th centuries, when the Hungarian city of Kocs, located about 70 kilometers from Budapest, (between Vienna and Pest), became very popular. Kocs became an obligatory stop for all trips between these two capitals. In this way it began to become very common to use a carriage characterized by being the only one provided with a suspension system for such trips.

In addition, it stood out for its comfort in front of the traditional carriages. Thus began to speak of the kocsi szekér, or "the Kocs carriage", symbol of excellence.

In this way, the term kocsi passed to German as kutsche, to Italian as cocchio and to Spanish as a car. In Serbo-Croatian, kocsikázik is used to describe the action of a car ride. Therefore, the word coach (car) is of Hungarian origin. It designated a vehicle thrown by animals to transport people, as Luis de Ávila states in 1548 (Germany War): "He went to sleep in a covered car, which in Hungary they call a car". From the city Kocs, the word kocsi (pronounced cochi) was formed. In a Fonseca work of 1569, "coche" appears integrated into the Spanish lexicon, as attested by the Diccionario de Autoridades (1729, v.). This is how the word "coach", derived from "car", and fulfilled the function of transporting people from one place to another. Coaching, in some way, also transports people from one place to another. That is, where they are, where they want to go. The only distinction, within this analogy, is that the coach is not the one who carries the trip, nor is responsible for the direction and decisions that the "driver" (client / coachee) takes throughout the process.

While this analogy, typical of the term coach from its origins and even the practice of coaching, is revealing, it is not enough to define how our profession was consolidated. That is why below I describe synthetically the influences that throughout the history of human thought have become and consolidated what we now call coaching.

Clarified this point, it is necessary to review the influences by means of which, this action of guidance or accompaniment that today we call *coaching*, derives from thoughts, practices and actions in use already in ancient Greece and pervasive until our days. L. Ravier (2005), continues explaining which are the most important genealogical bases as influences of the Greek philosophical thought in the current coaching, which we have already mentioned when we review the subject of the mind.

These are:

Socrates.

The figure of *Socrates*[43] is the most referenced when we talk about the origin of *coaching*. The truth is that like him, coaches "we help our clients examine their lives so that they deserve to be lived". To achieve this, our methodology is based on the Art of Maieutic, through which our client finds his truth or truth (depending on the client's own worldview), with a practical function for his life. We consider, like Socrates, that there is no teaching but only learning, and this arises only recognizing that knowledge is not in the coach but in the coachees (clients) themselves. In this sense, coaching is an empty vessel where the more "open" coaching is, the more place we will give to work with the client's own knowledge. Otherwise, coaching will be limited and deficient.

Plato.

In *Plato's*[44] thinking, we recognize the structure of his dialogues, as primitive coaching sessions. One of the most obvious conclusions, from the analysis of their dialogues, is the importance of questions as a working tool that enhances conversations (dialogues), and that serve as a method for the acquisition of knowledge in our clients. Powerful questions and *active listening* are the two most important tools or skills that a coach must learn to become a true catalyst for the other. In fact, a large part of coaching training consists in the development and strengthening of these professional skills. Also, like Plato, we understand education as a character trainer. Our job is to be catalysts of self-knowledge, both spirit, body, mind, heart and social relationships of our customers. The knowledge of oneself is the framework through which our clients can access an extraordinary performance, product of a learning process beyond the technical and formal scope. Self-knowledge is transformed, in this way, into the real source of any coaching process. Plato disagreed in some ideological aspects with his teacher Socrates and yet he understood the value of conversations as taught by his teacher. We, the *coaches*, understand that *coaching* is not an ideology, but rather a method based on human relations processes that can work with people independently of their creeds, religions and personal philosophies.

Aristotle.

It is known that *Aristotle*[45], as a realist, is diametrically opposed to the idealist philosophy of Plato. However, *coaching* manages to integrate the ideas that come from both. For example, Aristotle has taught us to work mainly on the "appetitive intellective" level (honors, recognitions and self-realization) of man. It basically tells us that man can become what he wants, depending on the things he engraves on it. We can go from being, understanding it as "what is given to us" or first nature, to the duty to be, our second nature. From being (where I am) to being (where I want to go) there is a way to go, possible and with an end in itself. Following the same line, Aristotle has shown us that the pursuit of happiness (teleological argument) is one of the most important motivators in man, even in the twenty-first century. Finally, Aristotle, explained that the basic methodology to become what you should be, is the action (habit). The action, as we will see below, is one of the two sides of our currency as a profession. Without it, the coaching sessions would not make any sense. Also as De Haan & Burger (2013) point out, in relation to the origin of the aid disciplines (in this case coaching), the origins of coaching as a guide activity and help to others, date back to ancient times:

"... The discipline of coaching may seem very fashionable, but it has a long history behind it. Inspirational coaching conversations have been passed on to us from classical times, in the dialogues of Plato and in the letters of Seneca to Lucilius. The first coach appears in Homer's Odyssey, when the goddess Palas Athena assumes the form of a mentor to assist the mortal adventurers ..."

We share this opinion; that there is a tendency in man to seek help at important and crucial moments in life, where ideas are exhausted, options are exhausted (we hold that it may be apparent), and an innate tendency to help others when asked help, advice or guide. These seemingly innate and typical tendencies of H. Sapiens, we will analyze them in the light of humanistic Psychology, which since the 60's of the last century, proposed its own body of ideas about the balance we seek to maintain consistency with the surrounding environment (family, social, work, etc.) and the impulse (as an innate drive), to always seek to be better, moving away from pain and approaching pleasure; concepts previous to humanism in psychology, gathered in the Psychoanalytic Theory. But let us go deeper into the field of humanism applied to psychotherapy, converted into a method and an intervention technique, of which coaching has assumed as mandatory the skills (qualities) that those who initiate must develop and assume the enormous responsibility to help others, in their journey under the precepts of ethics.

Humanist Psychology as a reference framework for current

coaching.

L. Ravier (2005), collects these classical Greek influences on aid models, which we must still know superficially, from the most current philosophies such as the Phenomenology that we have already described in the previous chapter, to the scientific and positive models of the Psychology as a human science. In this regard, we will now focus on the very high impact that Humanistic Psychology of the 60's and 70's had on various therapies and help practices, and how he universally contributed *heuristically*[46] to generate new adapted counseling strategies to the needs of modern man, but which has roots in timeless (*secular*) desires for personal improvement and development.

Given the primacy of man as the central axis of coaching, his desire to improve and obtain greater independence, the need to be heard and understood, and the often urgent need to receive guidance on current or future courses of action; there is an epistemological compatibility between humanistic psychology (basically the one proposed by *Carl Rogers*[47]) and the coaching model introduced in the 80's.

Paraphrasing Ravier (2005), therapeutic principles and methods applied in coaching sessions, taken from humanistic psychology as *client-centered therapy*[48], frame the help relationship where *the person is the center of the process* that has as its goal, and offers accompaniment to meet the imperative need of man to self-actualize and perform fully, and that include the following elements and therapeutic methods applied during the process and their work sessions:

- There is a non-directive[49] model for coaching sessions.
- The counseling center is the person, not your goals.
- It is necessary to establish *rapport*[50] in the help relationship.
- The coach is effective if he has a set of qualities necessary for the process.
- There is a need to generate different behaviors.
- The person advised can set future goals, and this helps generate new possibilities of relationship and behavior.
- In the human being, as we have already described in the previous chapter (and endorsed by psychoanalytic theory), there are *innate*[51] desires to develop as a person, and desires to self-sabotage; these efforts generate, when they are opposed, an internal conflict that must be resolved in order to advance and progress.

The above is a summary of methods and varied therapeutic attitudes (skills or abilities), where the center of the intervention is the person as a client or patient, in its most intimate dimension, and where their fears, desires, frustrations and past experiences, play a fundamental role because they give clues for the aid process that seeks to generate new behavioral possibilities. As C. Rogers described, the scope of the congruence between emotions and behaviors is the optimum state where the full development of the organismic self, manifests and where the person unfolds his human potential, from an optimistic and positive perspective to himself or herself and for their social environment. These perspective, position the person finally, in a stage of wellbeing and superior development where the possibilities of harmonious coexistence that Rogers called as *fully functioning person*[52] are increased. This process requires from the therapist, three basic conditions: *empathy, unconditional positive acceptance*[53] *and authenticity or congruence.* Let's see why all three are necessary and why *unconditional positive acceptance* is key in Rogerian-humanist therapy, because the conditional acceptance style largely explains the current disharmony and disadjustment, and because why the skill to accept client's suffering in an unconditional way is a therapist's fundamental competence, which has been transferred to the coach frame of work of today.

You see, in the theoretical body of client-centered therapy, the person as a total organism, learned to reject parts of himself (the Self), in a relationship where he was disapproved or accepted positively and unconditionally, (that is, conditioned to norms, rules, patterns, expectations, preconceived ideas and prejudices about the way of being and acting), which altered in his mind, his self-image and his *self-esteem*[54]; giving rise to dysfunctional emotions in his psyche and in relationships with others. The attitude of unconditional positive acceptance is a necessary therapeutic competence to generate rapport and the necessary trust, so that the emotions and processes that are generating organismic mismatch (incongruence, maladaptation and in general an unstable and labile mental state).

This process of opening is totally *non-directive*, in the sense that it is not imposed or conditioned by the therapist, and allows a progressive unfolding of emotions and discovery in the client-patient. Learning to develop this skill, this therapeutic quality, is vital and central for both the therapist and the coach, which seeks to promote a productive dialogue, to find potential possibilities in the person and their environment. A lot of time and effort should be devoted, so that the therapists and the coaches learn to manage how to apply this competence in the help process, and to be able to favor the decanting of the patient's emotions, which have been hindering their normal functioning. Anyone who chooses to act as a *coach* must be sufficiently trained in this ability to generate the right conditions for advice.

As stated by María Angélica Rosso and Blanca Lebl (2006), quoting Volker, in Sánchez (1998), referring to the foundations of humanistic psychology. "... There are four aspects that give an account of the image of the person, which coincide and give belonging to this way of doing and thinking psychologically ..."

- *Autonomy and social independence.* The person as an active being capable of intervening in their own development and taking responsibility for their own life (Erikson cited by Volker, in Sánchez, 1998).
- *Self-realization trends to growth and realization* (Rogers, Maslow cited by Volker, in Sánchez, 1998).
- *Orientation to the goal and meaning.* All behavior is always intentional (be aware or not consent), which gives an account of a sense that constitutes us as we are. The construction of the ego and identity is directly linked to this point (Frankl, Fromm, Adler cited by Volker, in Sánchez, 1998).
- *Wholeness.* The human organism is considered as a whole that is linked to the whole. Feel, imagine, think, do (Jung, Perls, Moreno cited by Volker, in Sánchez, 1998).

-

Also, María Angélica Rosso and Blanca Lebl (2006), refer that Sánchez (1998) summarizes some precepts of humanistic psychology in this way:

- Take the person as a center.
- It turns against the classical scientific requirement of objectivity. Build your own model of human science, based on experience.
- It gives more importance to meaning and significance than to methodological procedures. It uses traditional statistical and validation methods, but subordinates them to the criterion of subjective experience.
- Contrapose to the conception of life understood as functioning, that of life understood as an experiment. In the first, it is validated from the outside, in the second from within the lived experience.
- All knowledge is relative, therefore invites you to experience, taking advantage of the infinite human possibilities of mental representation and creativity to expand our knowledge.
- It coincides with the paradigm called Holistic.

Let's review succinctly, some Rogerian techniques, which will serve as a guide to be able to undertake a process of helping others and ourselves, based on coaching and other psychological and philosophical support techniques as proposed at the beginning of this book, maintaining our promise of value to the reader. It is essential to know them, and more fundamentally, is to put them into practice and at the service of our own process of rediscovery and development, so that, as Rogers said, we take the step of "becoming a person", leaving behind, habits, emotions and behaviors anchored to imposed patterns (learned by the interactional mechanisms already described), and that have undermined our present self-image and self-concept, affecting the full deployment of the potential that we have. Let's continue.

As mentioned before, one of the therapist's basic attitudes is *empathic understanding*[55], which becomes operative or instrumentalized, by applying the *reflective listening technique*[56] through empathic listening, and which according to Julia Sebastián (2016) refers, basically consists of in the reformulation of what the client tries to communicate more clearly, excluding any interpretative element on the part of the therapist. This competence must be practiced, according to Sebastián (2016), to get to master it in its variants that reflect emotions, contents and relationships in the client's mental world:

- Elucidatory reflections.

  - *Ambivalent*: when the client has two emotional situations found.
  - *Immediate*: contingent on the expressed by the client.
  - *Summary*: small summary of what was said by the client.
  - *Bifurcative*: show the client two possibilities, two ways.
  - *Walker*: clarify something implicit, go a little beyond what the client has expressed.
  - *Gestalt*: state the opposite of the client's expression.
  - *Terminal*: at the end of the session, return everything said by the client in summary.

- Reflecting feelings or emotions. They aim to summarize the uptake by the therapist of the emotions implicit in the exchange given in consultation, with the aim of promoting an awareness of the emotional at stake.
- Reflecting using Icons. They allow the symbolization of an experience difficult to verbalize, through icons such as

metaphors, images, present objects.
- Reflecting by evocating past events. They seek to make present a past experience in order to symbolize it in the here and now.

A coach or therapist, by applying active listening in the process that seeks to establish empathic understanding with the client-patient (*coachee*), must attend not only to the contents revealed through the discourse, as information of various kinds that is It is necessary to bring to the field of clarification by the methods described (summarize the contents, summarize them, offer two alternatives on a topic, invert the meaning of a situation with a diametrically opposite view, show ambivalence about the situation, among others); but also to the emotions that are hidden in the verbal (*verbatum*)[57] and non-verbal language of the patient in the metacommunication modality.

The above are some examples to reference, and to serve as a guide to the reader for their practice, where they can develop those innate abilities to deepen the interaction processes in helping others and to enhance auto discovery; with the authentic intention of accompanying and facilitating the process of reflection, self-reflection, discovery and self-discovery, on new perspectives and possibilities, when it needs significant events on which it has decided or is impelled to focus its attention. These events could be loaded with meanings that have been able to alter the perception of oneself and the environment. Hence the relevance of accompaniment, to facilitate learning in self-reflection, to discover and generate future resources.

These techniques are the result of the research that Carl Rogers began, when he dedicated himself to investigate the conflicts of his patients, and for which he focused on expressive language (spoken and not), as a vehicle through which they put themselves. manifest for the interlocutor or therapist, the thoughts, emotions and feelings (wishes, desires, dreams, beliefs, values, frustrations and fears), that it is necessary to analyze and contextualize more precisely, in order to clarify their intentionality, and how these mental products, are linked, or are responsible, of the concept that the person has of himself at that particular moment. The described methods seek to help the patient to be more attentive, to become aware of how he maintains through language (and *metalanguage*), belief systems that have solidified in the personality and that may be blocking his full development.

As we mentioned, this skill is one of the most important to develop in *coaching*, as it will also help us to be more attentive to the contents, relationships and emotions that we convey in our discourse towards ourselves (our own thoughts, what we say to ourselves), and in our interactions with others. Only by "capturing" these contents that are hidden in the words (when metacommunication and other resources are used), we can identify them, isolate them, interpret them and address them appropriately with the intentionality that we want, which for the purposes of our proposal, becomes the analysis of internal and personal communication, as a mechanism of *self-analysis* in an exercise of independence and autonomy that is a stage of the *Positive self-applied Coach model*, which we propose as a liberating self-help exercise of control sometimes blocked by "Powerful others"[58], and which drastically reduce our personal effectiveness. We will review this more thoroughly, in chapter IV.

So I invite you to be attentive to the discourse that we maintain with ourselves (automatic and recurrent thoughts, fantasies and daydreams, feelings that predispose us to be happy, sad or aggressive, etc.). Take note (literally speaking) of those thoughts, take note of those ideas, take note of those beliefs that are projected in the *field of consciousness*, and that drive and motivate us in a positive way or negatively condition us. Do the simple math of adding up as many times in a day, an idea, a fear, an anguish, a particular sensation, that walk through your conscience; it intrudes on your thinking and intercepts your internal dialogue, restrains your will, paralyzes your motivation or stops your enthusiasm. It is highly recommended to make the effort to learn to *apprehend* (capture) those thoughts, those feelings, those emotions and learn to differentiate them from the self (I); that is, of my Self. They are part of my consciousness, but they are not my Self. I can come to believe that I am those emotions, those thoughts, those feelings, those mental constructions, those motivations; but it really is not that way, when I attribute those qualities to him and I identify fully with them, suffering arises as a way of experiencing the world. In the words of the Tibetan teacher Tsultrim Gyatso, quoted by Valera, et al (1997):

"... To have any meaning, said Self must be lasting, because if it seemed at every moment one would not worry about what will happen in the next moment; it would no longer be the "one" self. But it has to be unique. If one did not have a separate identity, why worry about what happens to one's "I", more than one cares about an alien self? It has to be independent, or it would not make sense to say "I did this" or "I have that." If one did not have an independent existence, nobody would proclaim the acts and experiences as their own ... We all act as if we had a durable, separate and independent self that we constantly worry about protecting and promoting. It is an unthinking habit that most of us would not normally question or explain. However, all our suffering is associated with this concern. Loss and gain, pleasure and pain, arise from our close identification with

> *this vague sense of self. We are so emotionally involved with this "I", so attached to it, that we take it for granted ... the meditator does not speculate about this "me". It has no theories about its existence or non-existence. Instead, he prepares to observe ... how his mind clings to the idea of self and "mine" and how his sufferings arise from this attachment. At the same time, look carefully for that me. Try to isolate it from other experiences. As that I is the culprit of the sufferings of the meditator, he wishes to find and identify him. The irony is that, no matter how hard he tries, he finds nothing that corresponds to the self ... "*

Very well, dear reader, we have traveled a wide and complex terrain, where several roads meet and then fork. On the one hand classical philosophy with its argumentative methods with the use of *logic*[59], *maieutics*[60], reflection to address human concerns, and on the other; modern currents of philosophical thought, which laid the foundations for scientific approaches, whose object of study has been man and his mental processes. This is how Psychology is born as a science, with the purpose of studying the brain and its products, behavior and its consequences, to address psychological suffering, the need for change and personal and social improvement; to provide knowledge and praxis in human progress.

If we make a summary, and maintaining the thematic axis of this book, which is no other than laying the foundations, so that from the knowledge of philosophy, coaching and psychology as disciplines dedicated to studying man; to be able to apply these principles and techniques to our own experience, seeking to increase our independence and freedom, taking control of our lives in a responsible, conscious and intentional way to be better; we see that only applying reflection, finding and practicing meditative mental states and investing time and effort in recognizing our thoughts, our cognitions and mental representations, our intentions and motivations, is that we can advance in the path of personal growth.

This book seeks to start you on that path, learning to walk a new route. The amount of change achieved at the end of the day will be directly proportional to the amount of will, effort and dedication that we put into the goal of personal growth itself. It will not come automatically. There are no fixed recipes and there is effort to undertake to achieve that goal. Let us always keep that in mind and move forward.

How does Globalization 4.0 or Fourth Industrial Revolution affect us?

To understand how global human culture has progressed, and how it impacts us as people that are no longer local but global, as a consequence of the deployment of the *Fourth Industrial Revolution*[61]; Let's read what Klaus Schwab, Founder and Executive Chairman of the World Economic Forum, says in his article "The Fourth Industrial Revolution: what it means, how to respond" (2016):

> *"... The First Industrial Revolution used water and steam to mechanize production. The Second used electric power to create mass production. La Third used electronics and information technology to automate production. Now, a Fourth Industrial Revolution is based on the Third, the*

digital revolution that has been occurring since the middle of the last century. It is characterized by a fusion of technologies that is blurring the lines between the physical, digital and biological spheres. There are three reasons why today's transformations represent not only an extension of the Third Industrial Revolution, but the arrival of a fourth and distinct: the speed, scope and impact of the systems. The speed of current advances has no historical precedent. When compared with the previous industrial revolutions, the Fourth is evolving at an exponential rather than a linear rate. In addition, it is disrupting almost all industries in all countries. And the breadth and depth of these changes announce the transformation of complete systems of production, management and government.

Likewise, Schwab observes an interesting relationship between technological advances and their impact on today's social dynamics and future possibilities:

The surprising link between science fiction and economic history.

The possibilities of billions of people connected by mobile devices, with unprecedented processing capacity, storage capacity and access to knowledge, are unlimited. And these possibilities will be multiplied by the technological advances emerging in fields such as artificial intelligence, robotics, Internet of things, autonomous vehicles, 3D printing, nanotechnology, biotechnology, materials science, energy storage and quantum computing.

Artificial intelligence is already around us, from cars and automatic drones to virtual assistants and software that are translated or invested. In recent years, impressive progress has been made in artificial intelligence, driven by exponential increases in computing power and by the availability of vast amounts of data, from software used to discover new drugs to algorithms used to predict our cultural interests. . Digital manufacturing technologies, meanwhile, are interacting with the biological world on a daily basis. Engineers, designers and architects are combining computational design, additive manufacturing, materials engineering and synthetic biology to initiate a symbiosis between microorganisms, our bodies, the products we consume and even the buildings we inhabit ... "

With the previous frame of reference, and before going into the next chapter, where we will explain how we can help ourselves with the coaching technique and other methods; It is important to highlight the role of communication technologies on people and their psyche, in various areas of action; as one of the forceful aspects of the Industrial Revolution 4.0, which has transformed the societal ecosystem, and is conditioning the nature of human relations. Of all this technological phenomenon, we are particularly interested in reflecting on the high availability of intelligent devices (mobile or not), which allow us to constantly communicate what we do, what we want and what we aspire to. As we already know, consciousness allows us to be connected with our Self as the axis of our mental (internal) world, and with the external world through the *perceptual channels*[62]; but, how are information technologies such as *social media*[63] a reflection of my consciousness? Can we understand social media and social networks as an extension of individual and collective consciousness? What relevance do these technological applications have for our well-being or for our personal growth? It is obvious that the interaction we are having with social networks, as a vehicle of agglutination of opinions, arguments, desires, illusions, fantasies and information of all kinds; in one way or another has conditioned our way of communicating. Virtuality has been given importance as a channel available to practically all people, who use it for almost any purpose. In the networks we reflect part of our personality, we make life with a virtual identity or "avatar", which as a "virtual or digital mask", and we make to the measure of our illusions, desires and intentions. This mask has some particular characteristics, which in most cases, shows incongruence reality versus virtuality with the person who creates it: *mutability, transience, aesthetically retouched, emotional lability, suggestive, provocative, cryptic and disappointing* (when it intentionally seeks to divert the attention or cheat). Let's ask ourselves the following questions, and answer with sincerity: With what intentions do we make a presence in social networks? How does what we "hang" on social networks reflects our true person (my Self)? Does that virtual identity reflect our most honest intentions? Are we making use of the "digital mask" to generate opinions that are not congruent with our personality? These are disturbing questions, with probably disturbing answers, given the pathological attachment that this can generate in people, when they assume this identity as their true Self, or as the virtual expression of what they consider to be their true essence or themselves. As we mentioned in previous chapters, the suffering that can experience from the people who thus work, comes from the poverty of self-knowledge, when the idea of your Self is very vague, weak if you like. There has been an identification with that virtual mask, which distorts its relationship with itself and with others. Hence the importance of analyzing the virtual-technological aspect as a product of the fourth industrial revolution, which, when merging diverse technologies, has opened a new space that has been reconfiguring the collective consciousness (and unconscious). In the process of sincere reflection to generate greater self-knowledge, the analysis of the intentions mentioned in the virtual world is one of the aspects that we will have to consider, under the proposed premises. The virtual identity must be a reflection vis-à-vis a self in the process of growth and development. Let's continue.

IV.

Self-applied coaching is self-help possible?

Self-applied coaching as an exercise of
independence and freedom.

At this point we already know what coaching is, where he takes his principles, because he drinks from ancient and modern philosophy (from the West and the East) some keys to understanding man and the mind and because he assumes psychology, some techniques and practical methods applicable to the aid process. The questions fit, can I apply those principles to myself? Can I take a more active role as a coach of myself? Is it objective and viable to assume my own help process from my own resources? Let's see.

We hold that yes. It is feasible and feasible to apply these principles to oneself. Self-help is an ancient practice (practiced by Greek philosophers and Buddhist and Hindu meditative schools) and we are convinced that with training and dedication and above all with will, we can take responsibility for our well-being, on our destiny, based on the practice disciplined of reflection and self-analysis. How ?, For this we will unveil the steps to apply the psychological principles that underlie disciplines such as coaching, but we already know are much more universal and ancient than they seemed to be, and we have collected in a method of what it is known as self-applied coaching. The reasons for this, we describe them in a row.

Let's start by saying that as Carl Rogers mentions, what we are today and what we can describe of ourselves to ourselves and to others, is the result of a complex process of learning habits, attitudes, behaviors and expressiveness of emotions and feelings that were "facilitated" by significant people who participated in our earliest parenting. The contents of this process, their meanings, their intensity and emotional tone, respond in turn to a chain of interconnected learning (interpersonal, interfamiliar and even intercultural) when mothers, fathers, relatives, caregivers, teachers, friends and related, they added in one way or another to our initial education from their own frames of reference (world views). This process could be conditioned or not, but if it was emotionally conditioned, it imprinted in our "mind" prejudiced patterns where the own identity, the own essence, the individuality and the own particular need (rhythm of learning and pace, *uniqueness*[64]), was relegated (obviated , secluded, neglected), in the background and was not taken into account as it should; with the sensitivity and respect appropriate to my particular way of being, ignoring my sensitivity, my speed of learning, my particular way of seeing the world, breaking if you want, these aspects of your own self to impose a pattern, a way of thinking, a way of feel and act before the events of life and how to interpret it; without opportunity to question them, refute them, argue or reflect on them; simply assume them as valid and true forever.

In this way, an identity was formed, a particular personality, with its beliefs, its values and concepts about how the world works and how human relations work (family, personal, love and work). This identity has been reinforced by the events of life, (when we contrast those patterns against material reality, strengthening or discarding the imposed filters) and it has probably served us to achieve things: academic success, making friends, falling in love, getting a job, participate in groups of diverse nature, in short, live in the social environment with more or less success or achievement (then we will analyze the relativity of the term success). That identity that defines us as a person and that we already know is linked to our conscience and our mental processes, helps us and facilitates living together or, on the contrary, is riddled with prejudiced habits and behaviors over others. When asked who am I?, we would be surprised that, at the age we have at this moment, we would not know how to respond accurately. But, even when it costs me a lot to define myself, to describe myself, for myself or for others; I am sure that my habits and behaviors (work, social, relational, etc.) speak for me and are a very good clue about who I am, what my person is like, my personality, what my identity is, what identifies me as a being different from the rest; which beliefs underlie and move my behavior, which prejudices guide my decisions, with what patterns (flow of ideas and filters or assumptions) of thought I make decisions, what values I practice in my actions. I define myself as acting permanently, I confirm my identity in contact with the world and society, I fight to get away from the flock and find a way of being and being in the world that stands out. As we said, all of the above is embodied in behavior, in observable behavior, in everyday acts; which, as is obvious, do not happen by chance, but are intimately linked to beliefs and values, which then form *attitudes*[65] (as dispositions that condition our thinking and behavior), which are then the filter to evaluate the circumstances, which have the power to trigger my emotions and that are the cause of the behaviors that I finally give to the world. This sequential pattern of thinking, feeling and acting, as the basic theoretical argument of *cognitive psychology*, describes the great importance and primacy of thoughts (*cognitions*[66] for cognitive psychologists) in the complex process of emotions (the basic ones of fear, love, anger, sadness and joy and the whole range of concomitant feelings, as rationalizations of those basic states but interpreted in the light of beliefs) and about behavior. There is still the discussion, about whether the continuous practice of certain behaviors, with the passage of time are consolidated as *habits* that then form *beliefs* (limiting or positive), or if on the contrary; from the repetition of faithfully and rationally believing in something, these thoughts progressively form *habits* of interpretation of the world that condition my *attitudes*, as mental and emotional filters that I use to decide which behaviors to deploy in the world. This we will see later. It seems necessary and mandatory, that in order to initiate myself in a process of self-help (or help myself), where I will use my own psychological resources to grow in my personal development, I must first recognize my own person (my *Self*). We saw that describing ourselves is not easy, nor is it a habitual task, and we only do it when situations in life confront us with the results of our actions. It requires a reflective effort, it requires stopping a few moments to see inward, collecting the most significant experiences through which we have set precedent of who we are, where we have tried to leave our mark, our *imprint*[67], somehow we have shouted to the world: this is me, look here I am, I do not look like anyone else, I have my dignity and I have my personality, my character and way of seeing the world that is only mine, no one else.

Positive Self-applied coaching, **what does it consist of?**

Summarized in a simple way, it is a method of *self-accompaniment* where the principles of *coaching* are applied to ourselves (*self-applied*); with all its *heuristic* capacity and that seeks to promote *transformational change*[68] in life (ways of thinking, ways of interpreting the world). Here we will review in detail why this type of change that requires reviewing habits of thought and behavior, is so challenging to carry out and put into practice quickly and permanently. From this moment, it is necessary reading friend to begin to reflect and contrast these concepts that we will introduce, to better understand how they are created and reproduced in their own patterns of adaptive behavior, when they intend to initiate a self-revision, with the intention to change some aspect of their person; then the technique we will explain.

As we mentioned, there are no *magic* or *miraculous* formulas (this will be explained later with some recommendations of *Brief Psychotherapy*), to change our habits and behaviors, which lead us to be better humans. Only through *self-reflection* and unprejudiced and objective analysis (which are superior *executive functions*[69] of our mind) of our actions and of what we want and want to change is that we can move realistically and objectively in the path of personal development. The foundation of humanistic psychology applied to humanistic coaching, emphasizes making aware (from the preconscious or from the unconscious) the internal discourses and mental patterns of information processing (which as we said are established from early learning) to be able to discern and elucidate its impact on the final behavior, and also its impact as a *brake* on the total development of the person we are; as C. Rogers says, not to deploy a simply adaptive operation, but "full functioning", exploiting our human potential to the fullest, but, what potential? Do I really have hidden potentials? Do I have those qualities? How can I fully adjust to the circumstances that pressure me and require my attention? Can I do it by myself? Without help from anyone? What is the method?

Let's look. If we know that *coaching* helps us to increase the knowledge about ourselves, which leads us to increase our personal, social and professional performance, and that this cycle results in a better quality of life, then we need to understand, what steps should we take to reach that desired stage of high personal quality, where we already overcome the imposed barriers, where we are free to decide for ourselves and where our relationships are optimal; reinforcing the positive meaning of life. It is the logic of personal growth, of adaptive transformation, of *change as a paradox*[70] that leads us to transform and rethink long-held *suppositions*[71], by others more powerful and adjusted efficiently to our essence and uniqueness. This adaptive change (we insist on its *efficient* quality), however, will show resistances to be implemented, since it moves the foundations of the mental structure on which we have been interpreting the world. In this sense and as proposed by Cook-Greuter (2004), can occur in two levels depending on their depth and adaptive power, these author mention that: *"... the lateral change is when the system of assignment of meanings remains the same, but new skills they are incorporated ... ", while vertical change is adaptive when a transition to a new system of assignment of meanings is found, and which indicates a change in the "how" we understand the world ... ".* We see that then the adaptive personal change as a goal of self-development, requires transforming the patterns by means of which we make decisions in life. This change is not easy, because it implies a conscious and sustained effort over time, which in the long run will modify my vision of life for a better (more *efficient*) or more *adapted* and adjusted to the present circumstances. It's a change to see the world; it implies changing the way of interpreting reality, hence its adaptive quality, which allows through a deep and honest revision of me, advance in relationships and therefore be better, better human beings. To reinforce this point, authors such as Hawkings & Smith (2006), refer that this process is part of what is known as a *"... second order change that triggers when the person begins to challenge their main assumptions within their system of beliefs and to see the world ... ",* cited by Munro (2012).

Given the importance of this process as a requirement to change, incorporating new forms of interpretation of reality and our *reluctance* (or *resistance*), to change our habits, authors such as

Bachkirova & Cox, (2007) and Rooke (1997), also cited by Munro (2012); they point out that immunity (as conscious and unconscious resistance) to change can be addressed and "neutralized" or "attenuated", with a method or technique designed to make explicit (bring them into the field of consciousness via the analysis of one's own patterns of interpretation), suppositions long held unconsciously (totally incorporated into our personality), proving their validity and meaning in the context of the person's life; against a vision or criterion that allows that person to let go those patterns that he has corroborated as invalid and prejudiced, creating in this way a propitious climate to conquer the long-desired change (and to which we strongly resist).

In other words, in order to make change effective, it is mandatory to bring to the conscious mind those ideas that condition my thoughts and behaviors due to their affective strength and roots in my beliefs. How to change beliefs rooted over the years and that have helped me to place myself where I am now? What arguments can change my ideals and patterns of interpretation of the world? What are the advantages of starting to see the world from a different perspective?

Up to now it seems logical that the goal of the self-help process called *Positive Self-applied Coaching* is to generate in us permanent adaptive changes that modify our way of seeing the world up to now (always valuing the weight of the beliefs and values that unconsciously predispose us), as the only way to incorporate new modes of thinking and behavior consistent with ourselves; using our reflective and rational resources. In this way and keeping in mind that it is required to have a method, a guide or a model that instructs us in the steps or activities that we can (and should) test to change, let's first describe what is a *change*, (personal, organizational or societal), what is its *algorithm* (its logic, its flow of activities or step-by-step procedure), to start on the path of being our own coaches, leveraged in resources that are ours and that are "asleep" or "anesthetized" by limiting beliefs.

Change involves modifying, reorganizing, re-arming, redesigning, rethinking, and we all know the resistances (we will see them in detail) that are imposed when we are invited (or when we self-invite) to change as a consequence of our dysfunctional behaviors and actions. Reinvent ourselves, assume new ideas and patterns of thoughts, new values and as an inevitable consequence of this, new ways of behaving or acting, we already know that it is considered a *transformational* progress, a *vertical* change, in short a *second order* change. It is difficult and challenging because the process of change is going to require me to modify, unfailingly, my belief system, my mental structure, generating a rearrangement of basic assumptions and values. When this happens, I will no longer be the same (will my identity change?) And if this process of change has the progressive tendency that coaching and transcendent psychology (humanistic, positive and transpersonal mainly) seeks, I will be at a higher level, I will upload a step on the ladder of growth as a fully functional person and adjusted to the family, social, work and universal environment (ecological and respectful of the cultural differences of the world). It is a positive change, it means to grow in personal development, to increase my adaptive and *recursive*[72] capacities (I will have setbacks that are necessary to revise and adjust), and without knowing it consciously, I will go through the *paradox of change* in stages of advancement and stagnation, to reorganize the ideas and evaluate progress, to then define new goals to achieve and continue to evolve. It is a *paradox* since the change is dynamic and static at the same time. Let us see the famous Greek legend collected by Plutarch on "The ship of Theseus", to better illustrate this process:

"The ship in which they returned (from Crete) Theseus and

the youths of Athens had thirty oars, and the Athenians kept it from the time of Demetrius of Phalerus, as they removed the damaged boards and replaced them with new and more resistant ones, so that this ship had become an example among philosophers about the identity of things that grow; one group argued that the ship remained the same, while the other claimed that it was not." This can be translated into the following question: would we be in the presence of the same boat if each part of the ship had been replaced one by one? There is also an additional question: if the replaced parts were stored, and then used to rebuild the ship, which one, if any, would be the original ship of Theseus?

Following Varela et al (1997) on this *paradoxical* fable, these cognitive researchers mention that philosophers responded ambivalently to these questions:

"... And philosophers, being more insightful than most of us, respond shrewdly that there is no unique answer every-thing depends on what we want to say. In a sense, yes, it is the same ship; in another sense, no, it is not the same ship. It depends on our identity criteria. For something to be the same (to have a model or invariable form) must undergo some change, otherwise we could not recognize that it has remained the same. Conversely, for something to change, there has to be an implicit permanence that acted as a point of reference to judge that there was a change."

We can ask ourselves: Will my identity change if I change my old patterns of thought and behavior? As in the ship of Theseus, if I replace a wooden board and then another and another, or for the case at hand, if I change my thoughts, my judgments, my habits and dysfunctional behavior, am I still the same? I'm the same person? Do I keep my initial identity? Let's analyze carefully because if I would be replacing my past identity with a new one more efficient. If we hold that identity is an internal condition, self, maintained in my mind and in my consciousness, associated and linked to memories and memories, the question is, do I lose my identity, if I lose my memories and my memory? We can say that it is a medical and psychological fact that if a person suddenly loses his memory (due to traumatic causes such as accidents involving the brain, its cortex and its nuclei), or progressively (Alzheimer's and other *neurodegenerative* syndromes), it shows signs of disorientation with respect to itself and the surrounding environment; he no longer recognizes himself as the person he was, nor does he recognize the close and habitual people of his environment; in some way, the habits and memories that gave it a specific personality disappeared, giving way to a different personality.

We assume that my *psychological identity* resides in the brain nuclei, and if these nuclei are affected, that quality is also affected. The physically understood identity (height, weight, name, age, color of hair and eyes, etc.) is maintained, but the psychological features that give me a specific identity (such as personality traits that include interests, preferences, my styles of communication, my character, etc.) disappear or suddenly, or progressively, conferring a new identity. But that happens in traumatic cases like those described and for the purpose of this book and the path of personal change, the question about personal transformation and its impact on my identity has another approach. It is clear that if I change progressively (since changing habits and ways of valuing the world is a progressive and *self-actualizing* process), habits of thoughts, schemes of analysis and ways of valuing the events of life, then I am giving way to new forms of behavior that as we said, will consolidate a different way of acting, and therefore a new identity, objectively perceived by my environment. It is a dynamic and progressive process that, as proposed by UNDP[73], has the *synergistic*, *complex* and *paradoxical* qualities, as well as *recursive* (review of errors and achievements to improve efficiently) typical of the phenomenon of human development, with advances and setbacks to move from a current way of being in the world (*status quo*) to another more adapted where I can unfold my potential, when I acquire new skills where my individuality and personal integrity are shown in full.

How can this upward process of human development occur? To change my attitudes and behaviors for others more *efficient* and *adjusted* harmoniously to the family, work or social environment, is it necessary to move and then stabilize myself at some point of the journey? Let's see this. If the process of personal improvement requires changing habits of thought in the first place (change of *second order*) to be able to start issuing behaviors more adjusted to the environment, this means that the change in itself, pre-scribes to assume and learn new patterns of analysis for incor-porate them into my repertoire, which implies acquiring a new information processing scheme that must be stable over time, at least while serving *efficiently*; that then with the passage of time and in view of the results that are generated, it must be *reviewed*, *evaluated*, to *redesign* new ways of thinking and feeling that take us to the next step of operation. It is the logic of human progress. To propose new paradigms that with the passage of time, will give way to more efficient ones and so on.

For this reason, the process of *change*, both personal, organiza-tional and societal, seems contradictory (*paradoxical*) when it proposes that change implies *destabilization* and *stabilization* at the same time, which implies *thawing* (destabilizing, removing, agitating, energizing) current ways of seeing the world, to move towards new schemes of thought (in this case practicing new ways of analyzing, thinking, reflecting) on one's own behavior and its effects (as it helps me assertively and efficiently achieve my vital purposes in a responsible manner with the environment) in the medium and *refreeze* (consolidate, stabilize, institutionalize) these new patterns, so that they become effective in our daily becoming; incorporating ourselves as a new habit fully consolidated.

Here it is recommended that we remember the process long debated in the *social sciences*, about how new habits of thought and behavior are acquired. Recall the *linear* sequence of thought (cognition) - emotion (feeling) - behavior (visible attitude). This logical sequence, this *algorithm* if you want, has and looks for consequences in the environment that surrounds us. Let's see, if we think we want to drink a glass of water, because the biological system gave me the signal that indicates thirst, because that thought is oriented to search (in the refrigerator, water dispenser, bottle, convenience store, etc.) a sip of water The action of looking for water did not occur in a disconnected way from biological processes, thought processes, emotions and our behavior. This action that originated at the cellular level, triggered a process in the neural network to reach the *neocortex*, to evaluate options and alternatives, weighed by several filters (including emotional) that should result in the final decision about when, where and how much water to take. It means that we have a way of processing the impulse-state of thirst when that signal reaches the cerebral cortex, to finally become an observable and tangible behavior, with consequences in the material world. Now, we have been talking about higher level (*executive*) functions such as *reflecting, reasoning, meditating, planning, deciding, organizing*, which logically are used to assess the actions we are going to undertake after deciding how, when, where, how much, for what, why, with what. These functions, we use them to make decisions about ourselves evaluating their convenience, advantages, material and emotional costs, etc. that result in adaptive and efficient behaviors for our purposes. But this is not always the case and we know that the poor personal efficiency to relate, adjust to the environment, participate productively in groups, achieve our dreams, goals and objectives, is affected by the poor use of these cognitive and emotional resources that we all possess and we exhibit, but from which we do not extract its best power to achieve better human results.

By conducting a *retrospective* analysis of our personal, social and work achievements; we realize that not all times we make the best decisions, that we obfuscate or block and let the emotions decide for us, affecting as we have seen, our concept about ourselves, our *self-esteem*, our *self-image* in one sense or another . Why do we reason in this way that led us to make decisions or right or erratic? Why do we decide to accept a high emotional cost for ourselves and for those around us?

No doubt we can find an answer in the "form" as we process the information that we had at hand at that moment, applying the filters and paradigms already described. But let's stop in the "form". By form, we understand the process or flow of activities and steps that are taken to reach the decision making about what concerns us as people. This tour (which is undoubtedly an *algorithm* of the human neural network, which is to emulate mathematically with the algorithms of the AI[74]) we must detail and shred so that we are clear that *how*, *when* and *why*, occur within us and that gives us clues where we can and must make adjustments to replace them with new paradigms more efficient, that lead us to produce increasingly free and adaptive "decisions".

Notice that we are highlighting the word *decision*. At the end of the day, we urgently need to "decide". It is the result to which we wish to arrive after analyzing, filtering and evaluating our past actions, present and future to change, to improve. We know it is not easy, let's see why. Following Paul Watzlawick, Weakland & Fish (1974), the process of human change implies *"... modifying the frame of reference from where we place ourselves to look and define the problem or ...". Watzlawick et al (1974), invite us to make a vertical change, radical if you will, breaking personal and social myths like that "to solve a problem or situation, it is a requirement to understand its why"*.

Clarifies Watzlawick et al (1974), that it is necessary to reverse the process of analysis and challenge it, *challenging* ourselves, when instead of asking ourselves, why are we where we are, we question ourselves asking "... what is here and now serves to perpetuate the problem? And what can be done here and now to effect the change? ..." Powerful questions that if we apply them efficiently, we will be able to find varied and better adjusted alternatives to turn them into concrete and pragmatic action plans that take as point of reference , elements and causes accessible to our analysis. Undoubtedly, focusing on more precise *causes*, we can mitigate more efficiently the *consequences* we want to change, eliminate or create. We will detail this process step by step later. But we know that by approaching not from *intuition*[75] as common sense, but *counterintuitively*[76] the problem or challenging situation, we find that erring and failing are part of the road to achieving the goal; This is *paradoxical* and hence its strong roots as personal paradigms, that is to say; as to advance I have to change and as I change I strengthen my development. All this assuming the process as a *recursive* (and ascending) spiral of *self-*

observation, which generates *readjustment* and rethinking of principles and patterns assumed to be valid, with the ability to yield a less biased perspective, and with sufficient courage to promote high-quality human and social behaviors, relational and therefore, promote personal progress. It is a new sequence, already detached from old habits and patterns of thought and behavior, which have not been very useful for me to advance in the human and personal sense. We can say that it is a pending assignment and that if we have a clear will to improve, we will achieve it by ourselves. There are too many examples of personal improvement in the face of adversity. Let us be one more and let's see how we can achieve it.

Positive Self-applied Coaching as a tool for personal evolution.

We propose a *model of help* to break with the habits of thought that have hindered personal development, maintaining *toxic* and *disharmonic* relationships, charged with negative affectivity, where the communicational plane (verbal and non-verbal or as Watzlawick, digital and analog) perspire a underlying conflict (in our interior and in relation to the outside world). This model can be *self-applied* and is based on the intrinsic potentials of every person:

- Ability to establish *synergies* or productive and enriching contacts of the experience that result in learning social skills of personal growth.
- The *innate* capacity of the brain to interpret the communication process at all levels (of content and relationship, or in other words, what is said, and what is wanted to be understood) in relation to others and in our speech internal (that we say to ourselves and with what affective quality we do it through our thoughts and ideas).
- The ability to project our ideas into the future using *imagination* and *creativity* based on the implicit curiosity of man about the physical world and about the ideas.
- The need for *self-actualization* or progress.
- The ability to review errors, correct them and apply internal readjustments (thoughts, attitudes, habits, etc.) that empowers us to make increasingly accurate decisions.
- *Freedom of choice* as a dignifying condition for humanity.

These innate principles and conditions of man, are the foundation to want to progress always in an upward path, which has led the human species to the level of current technological development, but walking much slower in the path of moral and ethical development. However, it is necessary to initiate the reflection that takes us to a level of consciousness *higher* than the current one, where we make aware these deficiencies (learned and already explained), to take control responsibly of our mind and, therefore, of our life in the social context. Now, why do we say that coaching can be a way to achieve the above? Being as we already know coaching a method that seeks to accompany the process of learning and personal efficiency, it is logical that this method has the capabilities to apply it to varied situations, and for our case, self-applied following a sequential route (not necessarily linear), to be able to initiate it with a minimum degree of *autonomy*, which will progressively build our *self-confidence* in internal resources, and will give us greater *freedom of choice* when facing situations that require us to stop, reflect, correct and initiate sustained changes.

Posed as a *flow of activities* (in a flow of activities step by step), necessary to initiate the process of personal change, applying of varied methods and techniques (borrowed from psychology, philosophy, coaching, neurosciences, oriental disciplines and systems theory), is a recursive *algorithm* and therefore efficient, with the following sequence:

1. **Situation that monopolizes my attention** (It can be of conflict or internal tension or of social-emotional mismatch). It is important to clarify two types of situations.
    a. **Situation type A**, where the tension or mismatch is generated by me. I am the generator of tension by action or by omission.
    b. **Situation type B**, where I receive the impact of the action or omission of others in an unscrupulous, irresponsible and insensitive to the other.

2. **I review causes of conflict or mismatch.** In the case of Type A situations, search for "data" that supports those causes that lead me to clarify my level of responsibility in the situation. By data, we understand prejudiced information or not that indicates possible causal relationship with the situation (prejudiced learning, errors of appreciation or interpretation of the situation, distorted habits of thought,

memory failures, fantasies or ideas outside the contextual reality, underestimation of the power of the situation to affect us and / or the environment, lack of interest in facing the situation as a way to maintain the current state of affairs - status quo, mishandling of emotions, erratic behavior, clear communication failures, etc. .). The responsibility is defined in the next step. This procedure can be applied to Type B situations, valuing how the other uses deviant patterns of thought and behavior. The idea is to separate responsibilities as generating entities of conflict. From here, the treatment of the situation is different. We will see it in step 5.

3. **Do I have responsibility for these causes?** It is obvious that in Type A situations, I am responsible, so it is a requirement to honestly acknowledge my responsibility for the causes that generate conflict. So far we are contributing at this time to maintain the situation. It does not matter at this time to determine its primary origin, its root cause. For the moment, focus on how we are contributing in different ways to create, sustain or increase the situation. It is precisely these "different ways" that we have to put under the lens of sincere and honest analysis, to know where we will direct the effort of personal change. This approach will then be tested against the situation.
   a. **If I have responsibility: continue to step 4 ...**
   b. **b. I have no responsibility**: I value the need to intervene in the solution or to leave aside my participation, given the little or no influence on my part to change it.

4. **I analyze possible alternatives of attenuation or intervention of the causes** (for situations Type A and situations Type B alike):
   a. Verifying if I can help myself, or I need help from another person, to reduce the mismatch considered as

conflictive: within the potential range of alternative solutions and intervention of the situation, I will have to make an honest balance again, about whether I have the capacity to produce those alternatives with my own resources (we start as we already know the assumption of self-actualization, and the human potential to progress that is innate and that all humans have available). If I consider that I have the appropriate tools to successfully intervene in the situation and produce an efficient result, I continue to step 5 ...

b. If at the moment, I will need external help to generate alternatives that help reduce or eliminate the disharmony that monopolizes my time and attention. If I consider that I require emotional support and intellectual support to produce efficient alternatives, I look for the time, the person or group and the resources to support me.

5. **I propose change alternatives with self-analysis to generate a viable Action Plan**: for Type A situations, the alternatives to be proposed are goals of change oriented to personal development, so the alternatives will be very different from Type B situations, where I seek to understand with the tools of self-applied coaching, which causes the tension situation to validate if my intervention is possible or it is necessary to get away from the conflictive situation, to avoid further damage to my integrity. This step is perhaps the most important, given that it confronts me with the assumptions, patterns and models learned that we have already described and that introduce prejudices in my way of thinking, which trigger negative feelings and disharmonious behaviors. As Paul Watzlawick (1974) says, we need to change the frame of reference from which we place ourselves to evaluate something. And as Peter Senge (1990, 2005) says, to break the

paradigm that has not been to us to advance to a new way of approaching the issues, leveraged in the systemic or totalizing thought. Senge (1990; 2005), proposes the second of the five disciplines (developing personal mastery or personal mastery, identifying and developing our mental models, promoting shared vision, fostering teamwork and generating systemic thinking), as a pragmatic tool for identify mental models (which we already know are assumptions, *learned patterns*, common *errors of appreciation* of reality, *blockages*, *self-sabotage* and various types of *prejudiced paradigms* about the world); with which to practice other forms of thinking, mainly by applying the following:

• Review if we use the style of *jumping to the conclusions* in a hurried way, making use of a failed abstraction of the situations that require our reflection. This pattern, as is logical, will lead me to move ahead erratically in the decision-making process with the expected negative consequences.

• Make conscious what we shut up. Since these models are unconscious, they escape our rational judgment and the scrutiny of the intellect to take on a life of their own, dominating our perception by being powerful evaluative filters on situations and people. An honest reflection, centered on what we do not say and that are internal discourses (sometimes automatic and persistent), brings to our conscience distortions, false ideas and deviant judgments that we must replace to be able to advance. There is the essence of personal change. We have sufficiently stressed so far that only by modifying deeply-rooted thought patterns is the only way to change. Let's continue...

• Ask how you get to the opinion about something or someone. As other people come to develop their personal opinions about others, including us. How opinions are formed, what mechanism is put in place so that we have a particular opinion about something or someone? Interesting aspect that we have to clarify in order to introduce changes in our mental models, specifically in the process of forming our opinions about the world and about ourselves.

Given the above, we can bring together some ideas about the progressive and sequential qualities of human development, and some positions we have to take to change:

- Face the *resistances* that make us *immune* to change (Kegan & Lahey, 2009), trying new ways of approaching the problem or issue.
- Overcoming personal *myths* of disability and disapproval.
- Generating creative alternatives that produce *vertical change* (*second order*) and that are realistic to the environment and the available resources.
- Applying *systemic thinking*[77]:
    - Defining the problem or issue well,
    - Investigating their qualities,
    - Defining the change that is needed in a clear and realistic way,
    - Making a plan of action and putting into practice the plan.

- This scheme will lead us to *test* its capacity to generate the desired change, if it worked and if it was effective to correct it when necessary, make adjustments and move forward until consolidating the desired change.
- All of the above produces personal *learning* of new mental models, which generate *new meanings* about our potential, and in this way we acquire additional abilities, by overcom-

ing problems or imbalances with personal efficiency, that is to say; this new way of thinking and focusing on important issues managed to resolve, mitigate or eliminate stagnation conditions.

This way of looking at situations of conflict, will need to be *tested* against *reality* and progressively adjusted, until the most efficient formula that produces real and stable change over time is achieved.

6. **I test the alternatives to produce the desired change:** Logically after generating the alternatives to approach the situation, having applied the described principles of change of focus, analysis of data on the possible causes, definition of goals of change, etc. We must test decisions in the real world. If, for example, we decide that it is necessary to introduce a different way of communicating, we put this new form to the test and adjust what is necessary to see the feedback we get. These adjustments will give us confidence in this new behavior and we will be reinforcing it by applying it efficiently on a day-to-day basis that is, improving our relationships by having a more harmonious interaction. Thus, we are testing the new ideas and proposals of relationship and we are incorporating into our repertoire the most efficient. This does not lead to verify two possible alternatives:
   a. **The ideas and alternatives put in place worked:** If they achieved the objective of introducing improvements in the relationships and therefore better adaptation to the environment, we went to step 07 ...
   b. **The alternatives and ideas put into action did not work:** If they did not achieve their objective of attenuating, improving or changing the conflictive situation

(Type A or Type B), it is a requirement to return to step 04. Here it is necessary to clarify that this activity is recursive in the sense that seeks to review the failed alternatives to return to the generation point of the same so that other possible ones are generated and tested again in reality, until finding the most efficient alternatives, which for our case is the change of pattern of disharmonic thinking that generates maladaptive behaviors. As we mentioned earlier, the recursive quality of human development processes implies sequential progress, assuming setbacks and rearrangements that has been the result of an effort of self-observation, which produces change oriented to human development. This is a mandatory capacity of the process of change, which we must incorporate into self-reflection, which will help us to be increasingly efficient about our thought and behavior patterns. We could say that we are training our mind (we already know the main aspects it contains and defines) to be more precise and better equipped, to provide us with flexible and adapted ideas more accurately than before. The process of returning to the initial point, must generate new ideas that when tested and corroborated its efficiency, become results as described in point a, that is, achieved the goal of introducing improvements in relationships and therefore better adaptation to the environment.

7. **Consolidation of learning and stability of change:** Once the new thought patterns have been *tested* and their *efficiency* proved to achieve better human interactions, highly *adaptive* and harmonious; We began to consolidate a new learning that over time, should also be subject to revision and adjustments, staying in the recursive process of adaptive efficiency, calibrating each time the situation (Type A or Type

B) warrants it. The *recursive algorithm* in this case, returns to the initial point of confrontation of new situations that demand adaptive responses, but already with consolidated learning on how to approach them in a highly efficient way. If you want, we repeat the analysis of the *causes* attributable to us or not, as many times as necessary to arrive at an efficient analysis pattern and therefore to address the situation. As we already said, the *mitigation, resolution* or *elimination* of the conflictive situation is the indicator of the *efficiency* of *positive self-applied coaching* in an accurate way to achieve the goal of personal and human progress.

Very well, dear reader, up to now we have advanced in the goal of proposing an *efficient* method that *self-applied,* can help us face diverse situations where answers from me are required, that generate changes in my person, by incorporating new patterns of thought and behavior. We have proposed using logic, a flow of activities based on computer science (as *algorithms* and *flow-charts*), assuming the recursive, complex, synergistic and progressive qualities of human development, to propose a way to approach problems by supporting ourselves in efficient practices typical of *intelligent* systems. We could say that if we apply a more intelligent way of looking at situations, we will achieve visible changes that will lead us to achieve personal and professional development goals and we will be adding harmony to the balance of human society. From all the above, several conclusions emerge that are interesting to note:

- The situations that we face and that require our attention and *adaptive* response can be approached with different types of analysis, but as regards our own personal development, it is essential to apply an *efficient form* (with greater *intelligence* of all types), to achieve better responses with harmonic behaviors. We know that as biological organisms, our superior capacities determine the efficiency and quality of our responses. If those capacities are not applied appropriately (with discipline, parsimony and recursion), we will obtain painful and maladaptive results.

- To improve as a person, requires an effort to *analyze oneself*; that is causing stagnation, delay, imbalance and internal and social conflict. This analysis, in turn, requires directed and sustained effort to learn new models and patterns with which to look at my *inner world* and the *physical world*. If I do not change internally, I will not be able to achieve change in my environment.

- Sometimes, the situations we face, exceed our analysis and reflection skills, so it is always advisable to seek support (intellectual and emotional) to help us generate new ways of seeing the world. We find a natural coach in our parents, brothers, wife or husband, children, family and sincere friendships in our environment; Why not ask for help? That yes, following the recursive principle of change, that is, to test and revise to learn. That is the goal.

If we observe carefully, the flow chart or sequence of steps to *self-apply* the coaching to ourselves, we can appreciate two *recursive moments*. The *first moment* is given, when we do not find feasibility (feasibility of application in reality) to the proposals analyzed, so it is necessary to repeat the process, as many times as necessary to find a realistic proposal and adjusted to the situation. The *second moment* is when not having achieved the expected result, when applying the alternatives of confrontation or solution, we must repeat the analysis (applied to myself or applied to situations outside of me), until an efficient alternative is achieved, that is, produce other alternatives that if they manage to mitigate the source of conflict in a responsible and respectful way, to consolidate the learning of new paradigms or frames of reference, about ourselves or the social world. This is the nature of the *self-help* process. We can go through this process by ourselves, or we can rely on other resources to achieve the resolution of situations and consolidate personal learning and greater human development. Instinctively, our brain will improve in its analytical dynamics and will provide us (even unconsciously) with efficient thoughts to solve the tasks ahead. But be careful, for this to happen, we must put in motion some fundamental skills; which? Let's see:

- **Will:** understood as the *intrinsic motivation* to take responsibility for my personal development. This is the most important quality (more than skill or competence) that we must practice to start the path of self-help and therefore of self-development. Without will, that is, without motivation; nothing different will happen. The will understood as the innate impulse of man to progress and overcome, "ignites" the motivation that triggers the mechanism of thought and behavior. There are no unmotivated thoughts, and therefore there are no unmotivated behaviors. It is an internal process that is not visible to others, but that our interior is like a fire difficult to extinguish that pushes us to want to do things. In our case, the *will to change*, to want to change with real interest.
- **Discipline**: when we need to *sustain* new ways of thinking and behavior. That is, the execution of these new behaviors in a *sustained* manner, will reinforce our new mental patterns. Only with discipline of thought (for example, when trying to modify prejudiced thoughts about something or someone, substituting them for others more objective and respectful of the other's condition) can we generate behaviors consistent with that new style of thought that will make us more harmonious.

- **Optimism:** A *positive* vision about our capabilities and potentials is necessary to undertake a sustained change over time. The opposite is the condemnation of personal and social stagnation. We share the postulates of *Positive Psychology*[78], which among others, proposes that interpersonal quality relationships contribute to psychological well-being and mental health, that *optimism* and *happiness* are shields against psychological distress. Likewise, a *positive* image of ourselves, promotes psychological well-being.

Applying these three basic principles, to the process of self-help to improve my human qualities and attributes, will ensure that the proposed change is successful and remains in time, since it is well known that change requires effort and dedication. A new way of seeing the world, with renewed courage and optimism, an effort that we will see rewarded when we verify in our relationships, more harmony, more adjustment, more empathy and better emotional health. We have grown as people, let's move on!

V.

Change and the struggle between *instinct* and *will*.

We have reviewed what the change process implies. The effort to expose areas of improvement, zones of conflict, barriers to personal development, mental blocks, errors of appreciation. The *will, discipline* and *optimism* required to sustain over time the efforts that reflect a lasting change, but always in review to mutate into improved ways of adapting to the environment; they should guide our action in the efforts to improve. Let's see why it is still necessary to know more about how we function as humans. We will review with a little more depth, which causes that the efforts to change are demanding and sometimes unfinished tasks, or success stories. To do this, we will enter a very interesting field, which provides us with light in the midst of the complexity represented by the mind, conscience and behavior and how they are linked to will and instinct.

Carl Gustav Jung (1934) argued that "*... all knowledge is the result of imposing some kind of order on the reactions of the psychic system, as they flow into our consciousness ...*" But, what does that have to do with *change, coaching*? And the *self-help* processes? When we mentioned before it is necessary to go deep to understand better and more clearly the origin of the resistances to change, of our internal struggles and the power of ideas, values, prejudices and mental patterns; we will refer to the mental world in its dimension, if not more mysterious, elusive.

Now, dear reader, at this point, it is necessary to clarify how these psychologically described aspects affect human performance in relation to their development as a person. As in our mind (our *psyche*), there are the impulses that motivate us to take the necessary steps to change, or how those impulses are barriers and obstacles that can forcefully block our desire to change.

C. G. Jung[79], makes it clear that the will is rooted in the basic biological process where proper *impulses* and *instincts*, does not exist unlinked to the organic, and we could add that it is an epiphenomenon of the cerebral cortex; but also clarifies that in the domain of the mental (*psychic*), the original powers of the impulses are attenuated when the will is exercised with sufficient intention and strength. This means that even when the will cannot "disintegrate" the instinct, if it can take from it its energy to *deflect* it or derive it to the goals of change that we propose. How? Through the freedom of choice that is proper to the will, and this freedom is exercised consciously. This is very important that we analyze, given that we are saying, that with the margin of maneuver that gives us freedom of choice, we are ultimately the sculptors and responsible for our destiny, the creators of our circumstances, the guardians of our welfare and our achievement in all areas. The questions fit: can I make free decisions at this time to improve as a person? What prevents me?

If, as we have already seen, the process of *self-applied* coaching to situations type A or type B, seeks to be successful in facing the challenges of life, it seems obvious that this will only be achieved by applying the necessary will through which we consolidate tangible changes in our belief system, our assumptions, our values and our actions. Address situations with a new "toolbox", with a fresh, different and innovative vision when compared to the way we have come "being". It is also obvious that if we cannot find efficient solutions to the challenges, something inside or outside of us is preventing us from doing so. What forces me to maintain the same thought patterns? What hinders me from learning new ways of seeing the world?

Being my own coach to change successfully, is the desired goal of autonomy, of self-sufficient personal achievement, that propagates me to the next stage, already more free, and more independent; exercising a productive interdependence, dignifying and honoring my individual person. Therefore, we wish in this chapter to stress the importance of change (which we already know is always *paradoxical*), as a property or quality of human growth and the progressive process of becoming a person, as Carl Rogers put it. We will go through steps identifying areas of improvement, areas of attention, and opportunities for growth in the human and personal, when we come across situations that always demand more from ourselves, much more creativity and resolutive resources. Not the same idea, not the same attitude, not the same feeling or the same action. Another, an attitude and a mental disposition that manages to resolve the situations confronted once and for all.

If we can find the causes of our apathy to change, to improve, and if once identified those causes we embark on the journey of change with sufficient will, overcoming imposed or self-imposed barriers and leaving aside those burdens that weigh us down, addressing the challenges with the right tools (in this case the coaching applied autonomously); we will achieve our most desired goal because we will advance, we will be little by little building an improved version of myself, more efficient and always resolutive. It is expected that by making these terms, these internal mechanisms aware, and if we begin to apply these logics, we will be on the path of improvement. This is possible if we can apply the will to change in its most powerful expression, will to sustain new ways of being, to see the world and to behave in the world, to sustain them in time, so that they endure as a trace of our presence creative, intelligent and warm in the human.

What we have reviewed so far, dear reader, shows that it is definitely necessary to apply a high amount of energy in the form of a *willingness to change* (motivation and impulse), to start the transformation in thought patterns, to modify habits and behaviors It is possible, it has always been possible and it will continue to be a human goal, given the innate need to progress. So it is logical that we have to dedicate time to know which barriers have been preventing us from changing, which have undermined our will repeatedly. Due to barriers, as we have already pointed out, we understand learned contents, habits, personal styles, ideas, fantasies, unattainable dreams, etc. that are firmly rooted in our mental structure. What we usually do is apply all of the above as a form of *self-deception*[80], as a kind of *imaginary reality*, of a *virtual world* made to our measure, tailored to our hidden and explicit wishes and desires, in an attempt, always failed; to avoid areas of conflict, gray areas that have become a burden difficult to carry and that in one way or another, call our attention. This will be explained in detail in the following pages. I ask you, dear reader, to focus on this point. It is perhaps one of the most important to unveil the process of stagnation and self-sabotage to which we have submitted and surrendered for years. We can rely on the description made by Moral Jiménez and Sirvent (2014), when they explain how self-deception (in spite of having a homeostatic and regulating function of mental integrity), serves in most cases, for the purposes of denying Evidence on the arguments, read carefully:

"... The lies and the normal or physiological self-deception are inherent in the human condition. They play a regulatory or homeostatic role in psychological protection (Taylor & Brown, 1994, Taylor & Hick, 2007). In this context, the word "lie" refers to the process of congruence or internal incongruence according to the response of a Subject to a need of the state of emergency; In other words, the issue is usually found through necessity. However, lying is a communicative and relational failure, which is not socially tolerated: the individual who lies is condemned and isolated (Smith, 2005, Monts, Zurcher, and Nydegger, 1977, Sullivan, 2002). While lying involves deceiving another, self-deception is lying to oneself; it is used to maintain false beliefs or illusions that are very important for the person. Gianetti (2000) describes self-deception as the process of denial or non-rationalization. The relevance, meaning or importance of counteracting the evidence with the argument. In short, self-deception represents an obstacle to authenticity ... "

They continue explaining the adaptive and balancing function of self-deception as a way of relating to ourselves and others, let's see:

"... Self-deception is not pathologically innate. Who can claim that they have never cheated themselves? We all have a level, some higher, lower, self-deception in the form of illusion, fantasy or natural conspiracy, which we use in our daily lives to interact with others. Several authors (Joplin, 1996, Mele, 2001, Taylor, 1994, 2007) attest to the homeostatic function of self-deception, that is, its importance to achieve balance in the subject. Positive self-

illusions play an important role in the maintenance of mental health, as well as in the ability to maintain good interpersonal relationships and a sense of well-being. Such illusions include overly positive evaluations of oneself, exaggerated perceptions of self-control and unrealistic optimism about one's own future ..."

Other researchers, such as Lemos (2005), report that Whiten and Byrne (1997) have called deception an inherent function of the human condition, a form of "Machiavellian intelligence". The latter say that:

"... Theory according to which primates have managed to develop various social strategies that are advantageous for survival, resorting to the convenient use of agonist or cooperative behaviors, as the situation requires. Machiavellian intelligence is a capacity that seems to have been induced by the need to dominate increasingly refined forms of manipulation and fraud in the social environment, and which manifests itself through the use of strategies of tactical dissimulation, lying and deception ..."

Continues Lemos (2005) referring to Smith (2005):

"... Machiavellian intelligence may have been the engine that pushed our ancestors to acquire more and more intelligence and to become increasingly fond of changing their minds, closing deals, bluffing and colluding with others; so he estimates that human beings are born liars, having developed much more sophisticated forms of dissimulation

than our closest primate relatives. But dissimulation and deceit to others would not have reached such orders of magnitude if humans had not also developed the ability to deceive ourselves. Self-deception helps us to lie to others more convincingly, and the ability to believe our own lies helps us to deceive others more effectively. On the other hand, it allows us to reach the degree of perfection of "lying with sincerity", without having to make a theatrical montage to pretend that we are telling the truth. This is the thesis of the sociobiology's Robert Trivers (2002), who argues that the main function of self-deception is to be able to deceive others more easily, because the credulity in the story itself makes it more convincing for others ..."

But, how to link *brain, mind, consciousness, organismic self, paradigms* and *suppositions, lateral change* and *coaching, self-help* and its relationship with self-deception? Is it possible to advance and progress in the human and in the personal development even though as a species we are configured to deceive and self-deceive ourselves? Again, it is clear that if we can progress as people, always from the will as a key motivational element to "shoot" the attitudes oriented to progress. We have been progressively removing the process of helping ourselves by applying techniques of humanistic coaching, and with sufficient base in the analytical psychology (of C. G. Jung), in relation to the strength and energy required to initiate a personal change. It has also been made clear that the human being, we, each one; we are complex entities that respond systemically to stimuli that come from outside of us and from within each one, and that at this point, we can find a practical sense to all the mentioned, trying to pose an efficient self-help equation, leveraged or supported by philosophy, coaching and psychology.

We could raise it in the following terms:

> *As human beings and as people, we try in an innate (in-stinctive) way to progress in the personal and social, given that the demands of the environment ask us for greater and better adaptation capacities. We do this to maintain a con-sistent mental and social position, applying paradigms and assumptions learned and strongly solidified, that we put to the test, and that in that process of advancement, when these assumptions are replaced by more efficient ones; we find new meanings to the internal (mental) world and to the external one. We usually take small steps and achieve small successes, through which we progressively develop greater inner strength, greater adaptive power and an increasingly positive view of ourselves (of my Self, and myself) and the surrounding world.*

Thus, we see that there is a common thread that links our *mind-consciousness* with our actions (behaviors), and that in this pro-cess, activities that are alien to us occur, involuntary if we want, out of our reach when they are part of the "noise of background "which is already usual for us. Break that state to capture what is produced in that space, and how it affects me; It is the key to the self-help process, to apply self-help methods to be better. We have proposed the rationalist or scientistic technique of self-applied coaching, which from our left hemisphere in commu-nication with law, is capable of throwing efficient alternatives (emotional and logical) to address complex situations and to generate new ways of thinking and behaving, that little to little, they will train our capacities and bring out our resolving potential. As a resolutive potential, we must understand our maximum adaptive capacity both intellectually and rationally, as well as emotionally (*emotional intelligence*) and behavioral (comportamental).

But we must avoid continuing in the same state of affairs, so as not to feed the lack of authenticity, the impoverished vision of our capacities, the filter of self-deception, of self-deception that requires us to hold a *mask* behind which our true intentions are hidden, our true illusions, the authentic being that we are, that we always wanted to be and that we oppress involuntarily with an overwhelming hegemony. However, we can continue to apply other powerful tools that free us from those ties. We already know that the fundamental ingredient is the *will to change*, as the dominant power of volitional and compulsive impulses. Let's see what other techniques we can support. The proposal of Brief Therapy focused on solutions (TBBS or SFBT for its acronym in English) of various currents, widely known and successfully applied to various cases (from drug dependence, to family conflicts); It offers a group of powerful questions to which clients or patients must find reflective answers. These questions, always based on the rational and logical capacity of the patient, aim to activate a new way of approaching the situation. In the previous chapters, we already explained abundantly the importance of refocusing or reframing the problematic situation in order to find new meanings, and consequently, initiate a personal change with new approaches and assumptions for the future. So we introduce this specific technique of great success, given its connection with the *self-applied coaching* process, that is, we can equally self-apply in diverse situations such as those already mentioned.

If, for example, according to Sklare (2005), we are in a situation for which we think our adaptation or solution capabilities have been overcome, we can ask ourselves in several ways:

What have you done to survive this situation until now?

How have you overcome the problematic situation?

These questions pretend that we ourselves realize that we have sufficient adaptive, logical and recursive resources. That our distorted self-image (we already explained how we arrived at that personal fallacy), has prevented as a filter, gathering latent skills to initiate a change, in order to efficiently solve any personal, social or work challenge. By enunciating in detail and honestly everything I have done to survive the situation, come to my mind ways of thinking, attitudes used, actions taken, requested support, generated conversations, and proven behavior against the situation. This battery of options that we remember and take back to the present, by responding conscientiously to the previous questions, has been our particular way of approaching the problem. Let's notice that we also appeal to the solution formula of the problem, by answering how we managed to overcome it. If it is assumed that we have been facing it to overcome it, it means that we have the will to find a viable and efficient exit.

It is logical that from here, we must also identify those successful attitudes, propose to sustain the same competences in the future to be more and more decisive. We can describe that process like this:

- First we make *conscious* the *efficient equation* that has been successful.

• Then we reflect on how and in what way we have managed to *resolve* the situation and deal with it up to now, applying particular *assumptions*.

• We value that successful formula with other *paradigms* of ours that have not been successful in this type of situation, but that we can maintain or discard.

• And we *incorporate* (*learn*) those most successful aspects of that recursive equation to our repertoire for similar future situations, that is, we put it to use.

Another type of powerful questions, according to Sklare (2005), are those of the *"miraculous"* type, which seek to project in the future, a solution formula, always appealing to our recursive power. They may look like this argument:

Consider the possibility, that while you sleep tonight, the problem or situation that you have today, is solved during the dream.

When you wake up...

How will you know that a miracle has happened, and that your problem has been solved?

The idealized *"miracle"* or so conceived, lays the basis to begin to see the problematic situations with a new perspective, from a new angle. As if they had already been solved by applying a different and *efficient* approach or skill that we have, but that we had never used in such situations. This desire for improvement, supported by the creative capacity of the mind, projects the person to a new possibility, to an unexplored territory yet with an interesting potential. In a way, it pushes the person, if you like, to find alternative solutions created by herself, with her *own resources* and spreads to the immediate future, a vision of a recursive I, more confident in her abilities, more creative and wider.

Very well, dear reader, until now we have detailed varied aspects that impact our personal development. Some of them escape our will, others are totally manageable from our thinking. Applying these principles with great encouragement to personal improvement, is a task that will always yield productive fruits, both to us, to our loved ones and to the world. Many successes in the process of being a better human. Happy journey!

REFERENCES.

1. **Chaplin, J.P.** (1985). *Dictionary of Psychology.* Laurel Book. New York. USA.

2. **De Haan, E., Burger, Y.** (2014). *Coaching with colleagues. An action guide to one-on-one learning.* Palgrave Mcmillan. Bakisnstroke. Second revised edition. Neetherlands.

3. **De Laszlo, V.** (1993). *The Basic Writings of C. G. Jung.* Modern Library. New York. USA.

4. **Ferrater Mora, J.** (2000). *Diccionario de Filosofía abreviado.* Ed. Sudamericana. Buenos Aires. Argentina.

5. **Kegan, R., Lahey, L.,** (2009). *Immunity to change: How to overcome it and unlock the potential in yourself and our organization.* Harvard Business Review Press. USA.

6. **Lemos, S.** (2005). *Simulación, Engaño y Mentira.* Papeles del Psicólogo. Vol. 26, pp. 57-58. Universidad de Oviedo. España.

7. **Munro, R.** (2018). *Coaching and the Change Paradox: A Heuristic Study.* International Journal of Evidence based Coaching. Special Issue No. 6. Pp. 88. Oxford, UK.

8. **Ravier, L.** (2004). *Arte y Ciencia del Coaching.* Unión Editorial. Madrid. España.

9. **Rosso, M., Lebls, B.** (2006). *Terapia Humanista Existencial Fenomenológica: estudio de caso.* Ajayú. Órgano de difusión científica de la Facultad de Psicología de la Universidad boliviana "San Pablo". Vol. 4., núm. 1., pp. 90-117. La Paz. Bolivia.

10. **Sebastian, J.** (2016). *Carl Rogers: Terapia y Teoría humanista.* Recuperado de http://www.psicologiayconducta.com/terapia-carl-rogers-tecnicas, el 14/02/2019

11. **Senge, P.** (1990). *The Fifth Discipline: The art and practice of the learning organization,* Doubleday, New York. USA.

12. **Sklare, G.** (2005). *Brief Counseling that works*. (2nd. Edition). Corwin Press. Thousand Oaks, CA.USA.

13. **Schwab, K.** (2016). *The Fourth Industrial Revolution*. Recuperado de: https://www.weforum.org/about/the-fourth-industrial-revolution-by-klaus-schwab

14. **Valera, F., Thompson, E., Rosch, E.** (1997). *De cuerpo presente. Las ciencias cognitivas y la experiencia humana*. Ed. Gedisa. Barcelona. España.

15. **Watzlwick, P.**, Weakland, J., Fish, R. (1974). *Cambio: Formación y solución de los problemas humanos*. Ed. Herder. Barcelona.

---

[1] **Idiosyncrasy** is the set of ideas, behavior, attitudes, etc., particular and / or specific to an individual, group or human group, generally to another individual and / or human group.

[2] **Mind**. The organized totality of psychological processes that allow the individual to interact with their environment. For structuralism in Psychology, it is the totality of conscious experiences.

[3] **Structuralism**. System of Psychology associated with the teachings of Wilhelm Wundt and Edward Titchener. He argues that psychology is a human experience studied from the point of view of the person. The method of this psychology is introspection or self-inspection. (J.P. Chaplin, 1985).

[4] **Psychophysical parallelism**. Philosophical principle of dualist character that establishes an isomorphism between physical and mental events.

[5] **Isomorphism**. Isomorph comes from the words iso meaning equals and morphêque means form. Psychophysical isomorphism: Principle formulated by the Gestalt theory according to which there is a perfect correspondence between the physical

events of brain functioning and mental events.

[6] **Franz Brentano** (Boppard, January 16, 1838 - Zurich, March 17, 1917) was a German and then Austrian secularized philosopher, psychologist and priest, brother of the economist and social reformer Brentano Luxury and nephew of the German poet and novelist Clemens Brentano and his sister Bettina von Arnim. Disciple of Bernard Bolzano, defended the thesis of intentionality as a characteristic feature of psychological phenomena (as opposed to physical phenomena), giving rise to the so-called "Austrian school of the psychology of the act."

[7] **Edmund Husserl**: (Prossnitz, April 8, 1859-Freiburg, April 27, 1938), Moravian philosopher and mathematician, disciple of Franz Brentano and Carl Stumpf, founder of transcendental phenomenology and, through it, the phenomenological movement, one of the most influential philosophical movements of the 20th century and still full of vitality in the 21st century.

[8] **Empiricism**. With this name designates a philosophical doctrine and particularly epistemological according to which knowledge is founded on experience. Empiricism is often opposed to rationalism, for which knowledge is founded, at least in large part, on reason. It is also opposed to innatism, according to which the spirit, the soul and in general the so-called "knowing subject" possesses innate ideas, that is, prior to any acquisition of "data". For the empiricists, the knowing subject is comparable to a clean slate on which the impressions from the "external world" are inscribed.

[9] **Maurice Merleau-Ponty** is often classified as existentialist, due to his closeness to Jean-Paul Sartre and Simone de Beauvoir, as well as his Heideggerian conception of being, although later due to his litigation with Sartre, Merleau-Ponty denied membership or agreement with said philosophy.

[10] **Mindfulness**, also called mindfulness or full awareness, consists in being intentionally aware of what we do, without judging,

clinging, or rejecting in any way the experience1. It is a practice based on the concept of mindfulness or full consciousness of Buddhist meditation, and has become popular in the West thanks to Jon Kabat-Zinn. Despite being rooted in Buddhism, mindfulness is taught devoid of any oriental or religious component or terminology.

[11] **Awareness**. State of knowledge and understanding of internal and environmental states.

[12] Retrieved from Wikipedia.

[13] **Coaching** (*International Coach Federation ICF, or International Coaching Federation*) defines it as: Professional coaching consists of a continuous professional relationship that helps to obtain extraordinary results in the life, profession, company or business of the people. Through the coaching process, the client deepens their knowledge, increases their performance and improves their quality of life.

[14] **Barnum Effect** (or Forer Effect). It is the observation that individuals give high rates of success to descriptions of their personality that supposedly adapt specifically for them, but in reality they are vague and general enough to apply to a wide range of people. This effect may provide a partial explanation for the widespread acceptance of some beliefs and practices, such as astrology, divination, graphology, reading the aura and some types of personality tests.

[15] **Thought, Think**. The first as a concept belongs to the field of Logic, and the second to that of Psychology, insofar as, by means of the psychic act of thinking, thoughts are generated as timeless and non espatial entities. In short, thinking is a psychic act that takes place in time, that is formulated by a subject and that apprehends a thought, which in turn refers to an objective situation or objects.

[16] **Dissociation.** In psychology, the term dissociation describes a wide variety of experiences that can range from a slight distancing from the surrounding environment to more serious distances of physical and emotional experience. The main characteristic of all dissociative phenomena consists in the distancing of reality, in contrast to the loss of reality, as in the case of psychosis. Dissociative experiences are also characterized by the presence of a variety of maladaptive mental constructions in the person's natural imaginative capacity.

[17] **Nihilist delirium.** Delusion of denial, of non-existence. Term introduced by Jules Cotard in his patients who were later diagnosed with Cotard Syndrome. Patients show a tendency to deny everything to the point that they can deny the existence of themselves and the world. It is frequent in schizophrenia.

[18] **Immediate experience** According to W. Wundt, it is the conscious process as an object of study of Psychology, in contrast to the mediated experience, which is the object of study of the physical sciences. It can also be understood as thoughts or sensations without psychic antecedents.

[19] **Particular complex.** In psychoanalysis, they are complex based on an incident in the individual's life, as opposed to universal complexes such as the *Oedipus Complex.*

[20] **Identity crisis.** In the psychology of the Ego (I) of E. Erikson, each evolutionary stage (eight stages), represents a challenge that the Self must overcome in order to advance in a healthy and healthy way towards the successful and integrated adult personality.

[21] **Cognoscitivism.** Studies within cognitive theory focus on: intelligence, perception, thinking, memory, transfer, information processing and problem solving strategies, all of which are related to the learning process and teaching. Cognitivism has

its historical roots in England, towards the 1930s, when studies began on perception, thinking and other cognitive processes. Also Edward Tolman, at the same time, in the USA performs studies on the development of cognitive constructions.

[22] **Semantics**. Comes from a Greek word that can be translated as "significant". It is about what belongs or relative to the meaning of words. By extension, semantics is the study of the meaning of linguistic signs and their combinations.

[23] **Artificial Intelligence (AI).** it is the intelligence exhibited by machines. In computer science, an ideal "intelligent" machine is a flexible rational agent that perceives its environment and carries out actions that maximize its chances of success in some objective or task. Colloquially, the term artificial intelligence is applied when a machine imitates the "cognitive" functions that humans associate with other human minds, such as: "learn" and "solve problems".

[24] **Conscious**. Is a term used by Sigmund Freud, as an adjective to qualify a psychic state, or as a noun, to indicate the location of certain processes constituting the functioning of the psychic *apparatus*. In this sense, the conscious, along with the preconscious and the unconscious is one of the three instances of the first Freudian topical.

[25] **Unconscious**. In psychoanalysis, the unconscious is the key concept of the theory, since it constitutes its main object of study, and designates in the topical sense a system and a psychic place unknown to consciousness ("the other scene") and in the dynamic sense to the set of the repressed contents that are kept aside, apart from the conscience, even when they show a permanent psychic effectiveness and intense activity through specific mechanisms and formations.

[26] **Intentionality.** a characteristic of the acts of an individual that requires the individual to have goals, desires and standards; (b) to select behaviors that are at the service of reaching the goal

(for example, means for an end); and (c) call conscious consciousness a desired future state.

[27] **Behavioral Psychology** It is a current of psychology with three levels of scientific organization that complement and feed each other reciprocally: behaviorism, experimental behavior analysis and behavioral engineering. The latter also includes a whole range of technological applications, both in the field of therapy and behavior modification.

[28] **Behavioral therapy.** In behavioral therapy, the goal is to reinforce desirable behaviors and eliminate unwanted or maladaptive behaviors. The techniques used in this type of treatment are based on the theories of classical conditioning and operant conditioning.

[29] **Applied behavioral analysis** - ABA. It is the use of the principles of the psychology of learning, fundamentally of operant learning, to the modification of important human behaviors. Behavior analysts focus on the observable relationship between behavior and environment. By evaluating the relationships between a given behavior and the environment, behavioral analysis methods can help to change behavior. It is closely related to the fields of behavior modification and behavior engineering.

[30] **Operant conditioning**. It is a type of associative learning, this has to do with the development of new behaviors based on their *consequences*, and not with the association between stimuli and behaviors as occurs in *classical conditioning*. The term was introduced by the Psychologist Burrhus Frederic Skinner, although today it is preferred the one of *"instrumental conditioning"*, introduced by Edward Thorndike, for being more descriptive. The latter suggests that the behavior serves as an instrument to achieve an end and is given by trial and error, unlike the operative conditioning proposed by Skinner, which proposes that those responses that are reinforced have a tendency to repeat themselves and those that receive a punishment will have less chance of repeating.

[31] **Epiphenomenon** (from Ancient Greek ἐπί "on, in addition, next to" and Φαινόμενον "phenomenon, observable event") in philosophy is a secondary phenomenon that accompanies or follows a primary phenomenon without constituting an essential part of it and without apparently having influence. The concept of epiphenomenon is followed especially by the psychophysical materialism and the psychologists who sustain the somatic origin of emotion for whom the sensation of pleasure or pain of an emotion is the effect of a physiological change that shows it. They also consider the soul, thought or mind as an epiphenomenon of brain activity.

[32] **Broca area**. It is a section of the human brain involved with the production of language. It is located in the third frontal convolution of the left hemisphere, in the opercular and triangular sections of the dominant hemisphere for language. This region corresponds to the areas of Brodmann 44 (pars opercularis) and 45 (pars triangularis) and connects with the Wernicke area (the other region important for language in humans) by a bundle of nerve fibers called the arcuate fasciculus (or arcuato). It is named in honor of the French physician Paul Pierre Broca, who described it in 1864, after several post-mortem studies of aphasic patients who presented serious damage in that region.

[33] **Amygdala**. It is a set of nuclei of neurons located deep in the temporal lobes of complex vertebrates, including humans. The amygdala is part of the limbic system, and its main role is the processing and storage of emotional reactions.

[34] **Limbic system**. It is a system formed by several brain structures that regulate physiological responses to certain stimuli. That is to say, in him human instincts are found. Among these instincts are involuntary memory, hunger, attention, sexual instincts, emotions (for example: pleasure, fear, aggressiveness), personality and behavior. It consists of parts of the thalamus, hypothalamus, hippocampus, cerebral tonsil, corpus callosum, septum, and mesencephalon. The limbic system interacts very quickly (and apparently without needing to mediate superior

brain structures) with the endocrine system and the peripheral nervous system.

[35] **Bipolar disorder**. Also known as bipolar affective disorder (BAD) and formerly as manic-depressive psychosis (PMD), is a set of mood disorders characterized by noticeable fluctuations in mood, thinking, behavior, energy and ability to perform daily life activities

[36] **Schizophrenia** (from the classical Greek σχίζειν schizein 'divide, split, split, break' and φρήν phrēn, 'understanding, reason, mind') is a psychiatric diagnosis that encompasses a broad group of chronic and serious mental disorders, often characterized by behaviors that they are anomalous for the community and an altered perception of reality.1 Schizophrenia also causes a change maintained in several aspects of the psychic functioning of the individual, mainly of the consciousness of reality, and a more or less complex neuropsychological disorganization, especially of the executive functions, which leads to a difficulty in maintaining motivated and goal-directed behaviors, and significant social dysfunction. Among the frequent symptoms are delusional beliefs, confused thinking, auditory hallucinations, and reduction of social activities and / or isolation.

[37] **Depersonalization** It is an alteration of the perception or experience of oneself in such a way that one feels "separated" from the mental processes or body, as if one were an external observer to them.1 It can be due to the recreational use of psychotropic drugs , but more usually derives from anxiety, and constant emotional abuse. A person suffering from depersonalization feels that he has changed and the world has become less real, vague, dreamy or meaningless. It can sometimes be a very disturbing experience, while many feel that they actually "live in a dream".

[38] **Prognosis** In psychiatry, Prognosis or Judgment about the possible course of a disease.

[39] **Faith**. Belief and personal hope in the existence of a superior

being (a god or several gods) that generally implies the following of a set of religious principles, rules of social and individual behavior and a certain vital attitude, since the person considers that belief as an important or essential aspect of life.

[40] **Digital age**. It is the name given to the period in the history of humanity that is linked to information and communication technologies (ICT). The beginning of this period is associated with the digital revolution, although it has its antecedents in technologies such as telephone, radio or television, which made the flow of information become faster than physical movement.

[41] **Coaching**. Anglicism that comes from the English verb to coach, "to train") is a method that consists of accompanying, instructing or training a person or a group of them, in order to achieve goals or develop specific skills. While the term coach has a direct origin from the sports field and this in turn a means of transport Hungarian (kocsi secker), it is in the business and personal environment where it is known by coaching the dialogical and praxeological process by which The coach or coach generates the conditions for the person or group involved in the process to seek the path to achieve the objectives set using their own resources and strongly supported skills of motivation, responsibility and creativity.1 There are many methods and types of coaching. which vary greatly according to the philosophical school to which they subscribe. The person who performs the coaching process receives the name of coach (AFI: [koʊtʃ], "coach"), while the person who receives it is called coachee.

[42] **Epistemology**. The first step necessary when defining a concept is to determine the etymological origin of it. In this sense, we can emphasize that it is in the Greek where we find the antecedents of the term epistemology that now occupies us. Moreover, this noun is composed of the union of two words: episteme that can be translated as "knowledge or science" and logos that would come to mean "discourse". Epistemology is a discipline that studies how knowledge of science is generated and validated. Its function is to analyze the precepts that are used to justify the scientific data, considering the social, psychological and even

historical factors that come into play. In that sense, we can establish even more clearly that the epistemology of what is in charge is to approach philosophy and knowledge through the answer to various questions of vital importance such as the following: What is knowledge? How do we humans carry out reasoning? or how do we prove that what we have understood is true?

[43] **Socrates**. (in Ancient Greek, Σωκράτης, Sōkrátēs, Athens, 470-ib., 399 BC) was a classical Greek philosopher considered one of the greatest of both Western and universal philosophy. He was a teacher of Plato, who had Aristotle as a disciple, these three being the fundamental representatives of the philosophy of Ancient Greece. Socrates was a leading figure in the transformation of Greek philosophy into a continuous and unified project. Then, we know that he spent much of his life generating discussions with everyone in Athens, trying to determine if anyone had any idea of what he was talking about, especially when the topic was important, such as justice, beauty or truth. . He did not leave any writing, but he inspired many disciples. In his old age, he became the focus of the hostility of many of the city who saw the sophists and philosophy, interchangeably, as the destroyers of the piety and morality of the city; and was executed in 399 a. C. Details of the life of Socrates are known thanks to three contemporary sources: the dialogues of Plato, the works of Aristophanes and the dialogues of Xenophon. There is no evidence that Socrates has published any of his writings. Socrates was the father of political philosophy and ethics and is the main source of all important topics of Western philosophy in general; perhaps his most important contribution to Western thought is his dialectical mode of inquiry, known as the Socratic method or "cast" method, which he applied to the examination of key moral concepts, such as good and justice.

[44] **Plato**. (Greek: Πλάτων, Plátōn, Athens or Aegina, c. 427-347 BC) was a Greek philosopher follower of Socrates and teacher of Aristotle. In 387 he founded the Academy, an institution that would continue its march for more than nine hundred years and to which Aristotle would go from Stagira to study philosophy around 367, sharing, in this way, about twenty years of friendship and work with his teacher. Plato actively participated in

the teaching of the Academy and wrote, always in the form of dialogue, on the most diverse topics, such as philosophy-politics, ethics, psychology, anthropology, philosophy, epistemology, gnoseology, metaphysics, cosmogony, cosmology, philosophy of language and philosophy of Education; he also tried to translate his original political theory into a real state, which is why he traveled twice to Syracuse, Sicily, with the intention of implementing his project there, but he failed both times and managed to escape painfully and his life was in danger due to the persecutions he suffered on the part of his opponents. His influence as author and systematizer has been incalculable throughout the history of philosophy, of which it has often been said that he achieved identity as a discipline thanks to his works.

[45] **Aristotle**. (in ancient Greek: Ἀριστοτέλης, Aristotélēs; Estagira, 384 BC-Calcis, 322 BC) was a polymath: philosopher, logician and scientist of Ancient Greece whose ideas have exerted an enormous influence on the intellectual history of West for more than two millennia. Aristotle wrote about 200 treatises (of which only 31 have survived) on an enormous variety of subjects, among them: logic, metaphysics, philosophy of science, ethics, political philosophy, aesthetics, rhetoric, physics, astronomy and biology. Aristotle transformed many, if not all, of the areas of knowledge he addressed. He is recognized as the founding father of logic and biology, because although there are reflections and previous writings on both subjects, it is in the work of Aristotle, where the first systematic investigations on this matter are found. Among many other contributions, Aristotle formulated the theory of spontaneous generation, the principle of non-contradiction, the notions of category, substance, act, power and first immobile motor. Some of his ideas, which were novel for the philosophy of his time, today are part of the common sense of many people. Aristotle was a disciple of Plato and other thinkers, such as Eudoxus of Cnidus, during his twenty years at the Academy of Athens. He was Alexander the Great's teacher in the Kingdom of Macedonia for almost 5 years. In the last stage of his life he founded the Lyceum in Athens, where he taught until a year before his death.

[46] **Heuristic**. As a scientific methodology, the heuristic is applicable to any science and includes the development of aux-

iliary means, principles, rules, strategies and programs that facilitate the search for ways of solving problems; that is, to solve tasks of any kind for which an algorithmic solution procedure is not available. According to Horst Müler: "Heuristic procedures are forms of work and thought that support the conscious realization of demanding mental activities." Heuristic procedures as a scientific method can be divided into principles, rules and strategies. A scientific theory has a high heuristic value if it is capable of generating new ideas or inducing new inventions. For this, without being irrelevant, it is not essential that the theory be true or uncertain.

[47] **Carl Rogers**. (January 8, 1902, Oak Park, Illinois, United States - February 4, 1987, San Diego, California, United States) American psychologist, initiator with Abraham Maslow of the humanistic approach in psychology. A study conducted between American and Canadian psychologists in 1982 placed him as the most influential psychotherapist in history, ahead of Albert Ellis and Sigmund Freud.

[48] **Client-centered Therapy**. A form of psychotherapy developed by Carl Rogers in the early 1940s. According to Rogers, there is an orderly process of self-discovery and updating of the client in response to empathic understanding, acceptance and respect by the therapist of the client's framework. The therapist sets the stage for personality growth by reflecting and clarifying the client's ideas, that he can see himself more clearly and have a closer contact with his real self. As the therapy progresses, the client resolves the conflicts, reorganizes the values and approaches of life and learns to interpret their thoughts and feelings, changing the behavior that he considers problematic.

[49] **Non-directive**. Rogers and Abraham Maslow are considered the pioneers of this theoretical orientation. For Rogers, psychopathology is derived from the incongruence between the experience of the organism ("organismic self") and the self-concept, or sense of identity; thus, the symptoms appear when the behavior and the emotions are not coherent with the person's idea of herself. Consequently, therapy must focus on the client achieving

this congruence. When it does, it can develop fully, being open to the experiences of the present and feeling confidence in its own organism. For this author - and for many others after him - the effectiveness of psychotherapy does not depend so much on the application of certain techniques as on passing through specific phases and the therapist's attitudes.

[50] **Rapport** it is the phenomenon in which two or more people feel that they are in psychological and emotional "attunement" (sympathy), because they feel similar or relate well to each other. The rapport theory includes three behavioral components: mutual attention, mutual positivity and coordination. The word is derived from the French verb rapporter which literally means to bring something in return. Rapport is commonly established in the therapeutic introduction or in a certain social situation that merits a stimulus and at the same time an exchange of information, in which its psychological basis is established.

[51] **Innate**. Present in the individual at birth. The term innate does not necessarily imply that the behavior in question appears fully deployed without practice or independent of environmental effects.

[52] **Fully functioning person**. In a philosophical sense, person-centered therapists consider the human being as a person who, during their entire life, lives in an interdependence between their needs for autonomy and their needs to be related to others and to society. The two needs are existential. One of the goals of person-centered therapy

[53] **Unconditional positive acceptance**. Attitude of the therapist of total respect and acceptance of the experiences and feelings of the patient. Such acceptance does not imply agreeing or giving consent, but understanding that what the patient expresses is part of their experience.

Together with the empathy and congruence or authenticity of the therapist, it would constitute for Rogers one of the necessary attitudes for the therapeutic change.

[54] **Self esteem**. The degree to which the qualities and characteristics in the self concept are perceived as positive. It reflects the physical self-image of the person, the vision of their achievements and capacities and values and perceived success as well as the ways and ways in which people respond to that person. The more positive is the accumulated perception of these qualities and characteristics, the higher the self-esteem. A reasonably high degree of self-esteem is considered an important ingredient for mental health.

[55] **Empathic compression** It means putting oneself in the place of the other, capturing not only the objective meaning of what it says, but also the subjective and personal sense, the meaning that in its life has what it communicates. It is a specific quality of the mediator.

[56] **Reflective listening technique** consists of the reformulation of what the client tries to communicate more clearly, excluding any interpretative element on the part of the therapist.

[57] **Verbatum** Textual words of the patient.

[58] **Powerful others**. People who believe they are in control of their destinies have an internal locus of control (internals). Those who believe that luck and *powerful others* determine their fate have an external locus of control (externals).

[59] **Logic**. Part of the philosophy that studies the forms and general principles that govern knowledge and human thought, considered purely in itself, without reference to objects. "The main problems of logic are the doctrines of the concept, of the judgment, of the syllogism and of the method".

[60] **Mayeutica** (from the Greek μαιευτικός, maieutikós, "expert in childbirths"; μαιευτικη', maieutiké, "technique of assisting in

childbirths" 1) is the method applied by Socrates through which the teacher makes the student, by means of questions, discover knowledge. Like the midwife, Sócrates carries out three fundamental functions: it awakens and pacifies the pains of childbirth, it leads well the difficult childbirths and it provokes, if necessary, the abortion; the process is painful due to the cruel questions of the Socratic method, but this triggers enlightenment, in which the truth starts from the same individual. The technique consists in asking the interlocutor about something (a problem, for example) and then proceeds to discuss the answer given by establishing general concepts. The debate leads the interlocutor to a new concept developed from the previous one. In general, maieutics is often confused with Socratic irony.

[61] **Fourth Industrial Revolution.** The Fourth Industrial Revolution, also known as Industry 4.0 or Industrial Revolution stage four, is the fourth important industrial stage that has been verified since the beginning of the industrial revolution in the eighteenth century. This fourth stage is characterized by a fusion of technologies currently under test or in development, what is disintegrating the boundaries between the physical, digital, and biological spheres.

[62] **Perceptual channels**. Sensory modalities can include visual, auditory, tactile, olfactory and gustatory. Perceptual learning forms an important foundation of complex cognitive processes (ie, language) and interacts with other types of learning to produce perceptual expertise.

[63] **Social media**. Social media is a term originated in communication. These refer to the set of groups, communities and organizations linked to each other through social relationships. This was the result of the convergence of the media, their political economy and the development of technologies, with the objective of the interaction of two or more channels. Social networks are Internet sites formed by communities of individuals with common interests or activities (such as friendship, kinship, work) and that allow contact between them, so that they can communicate and exchange information.

[64] **Uniqueness**. The principle of uniqueness explains that each event, each event has the characteristic of its uniqueness, of its particularity. There may be beings, objects, people, events or similar circumstances, but never the same.

[65] **Attitude**. Rodríguez (1991) distinguishes three components of attitudes: Cognitive component: for there to be an attitude, it is necessary that there is also a cognitive representation of object. It is formed by perceptions and beliefs towards an object, as well as by the information we have about an object. In this case we talk about attitudinal models of expectation for value, especially in reference to the studies of Fishbein and Ajzen. Objects that are not known or that do not have information can not generate attitudes. Cognitive representation may be vague or erroneous, in the first case the affect related to the object will tend to be low; when it is wrong, it will not affect the intensity of the affection at all. Affective component: it is the feeling in favor or against a social object. It is the most characteristic component of attitudes. Here lies the main difference with beliefs and opinions - which are characterized by their cognitive component. Behavioral component: is the tendency to react to objects in a certain way. It is the active component of attitude. To explain the relationship between attitude and behavior, Fishbein and Ajzen, (1980, cited in Rodríguez) have developed a general theory of behavior, which integrates a group of variables that are related to decision making at the behavioral level, has been called Theory of reasoned action. Social psychology distinguishes a study of the intra-attitudinal structure of the attitude, to identify the internal structure, of a study of the inter-attitudinal structure.

[66] **Cognition**. (from the Latin cognoscere, 'to know') is the faculty of a living being to process information from perception, acquired knowledge (experience) and subjective characteristics that allow to value information. It consists of processes such as learning, reasoning, attention, memory, problem solving, decision making, feelings. The human being has the ability to know with all the aforementioned processes.

[67] **Imprint** is a term used in psychology and ethology that describes any type of learning occurred in a certain critical phase, whether in a particular age or stage of life, which is rapid and apparently independent of the importance of the behavior. It was originally used to describe situations in which an animal or person learns the characteristics of a stimulus, which is "imprinted" on the subject. Peculiar and distinctive feature that a person leaves in his works and that distinguishes them from others, "his style has the imprint of a great literary personality, he is a soloist who leaves his mark in each performance".

[68] **Transformational change** is required when there are alterations in certain areas caused by an interaction with environmental factors that create the need for new behaviors or paradigm changes at the individual, organizational or societal level.

[69] **Executive functions**. is a concept of the field of neuropsychology that encompasses a wide range of cognitive skills directed to the achievement of a goal and oriented to the future. Within the executive functions there are different processes that converge in their general concept, among them we can find the basic ones such as inhibition of response, cognitive flexibility and working memory, and those that derive from them, such as planning and organization. The executive functions allow responding to new situations and are the basis for controlling other cognitive, emotional and behavioral processes. They are very important for the execution of most of the daily activities of the human being, mainly those that involve the creation of plans, decision making, problem solving, self-control and regulation.

[70] **Change as a paradox**. Fritz Pearls described this paradox when he said that "change happens when we become what we are and not what we are not".

[71] **Assumptions.** Assumption is the realization of conjectures about something (facts, causes that have originated, among others), which are made based on evidence or analogies against

similar facts or causes.

[72] **Recursivity.** A recursive algorithm is an algorithm that expresses the solution of a problem in terms of a call to itself. The call to itself is known as recursive or recurrent call. According to UNDP, recursion refers to a change that is possible only in reference to structure (autopoiesis). Involving necessary setbacks for the sequential advance, setbacks that allow the rearrangement of the structure through self-observation.

[73] **UNDP-PNUD-UN**. The United Nations Development Program (UNDP) is the one that places people at the center of development. It deals with the promotion of the potential development of people, the increase of their possibilities, and the enjoyment of the freedom to live the life they value. The most important publication on human development is the UNDP Annual Report on Human Development.

[74] AI. Artificial intelligence.

[75] **Intuition**. The word intuition usually means the direct and immediate vision of a reality or the direct and immediate understanding of a truth. Condition so that there is intuition in both cases is that there are no intermediary elements that get in the way of "direct vision". It has been common to oppose intuitive thinking, discursive thinking, but several authors prefer to contrast intuition to deduction (Descartes) or concept (Kant).

[76] **Counterintuitive** A counterintuitive proposition is one that does not seem likely to be true when evaluated using intuition, common sense or visceral feelings. Objective truths scientifically discovered or mathematically tested are often called counterintuitive when intuition, emotions and other cognitive processes outside deductive rationality interpret them as incorrect. However, the subjective nature of intuition limits the objectivity of what we call counterintuitive because what is counterintuitive for one may be intuitive for another. This can happen in cases where intuition changes with knowledge. For example, many

aspects of quantum mechanics or general relativity may seem contradictory to a layman, while they may be intuitive for a particle physicist.

[77] **Systemic thinking**. Systemic thinking is the activity performed by the mind in order to understand the functioning of a system and solve the problem presented by its emerging properties. It is a holistic way of thinking that contemplates the whole and its parts, as well as the connections between them (Study the whole to understand the parts).

[78] **Positive Psychology.** Positive Psychology studies diverse aspects of the human being: positive emotions such as happiness, joy or love and strengths such as optimism, creativity, gratitude, wisdom or resilience. Recent studies have shown, for example, that the influence of economic income on happiness is only relevant to cover basic needs. From a certain level, higher levels of income do not seem to provide higher levels of happiness.

[79] **Carl Gustav Jung**. (Kesswil, Canton of Turgovia, Switzerland, July 26, 1875-Küsnacht, Canton of Zurich, ibidem, June 6, 1961) was a Swiss psychiatrist, psychologist and essayist, a key figure in the early stage of psychoanalysis; later, founder of the school of analytical psychology, also called complex psychology and deep psychology.

[80] **Self-deception.** Self-deception is the process of refusing to rationalize the relevance, significance, or importance of contrary evidence and logical arguments that are opposed to one's own. Self-deception involves convincing oneself of a "truth" (or lack of truth) that does not reveal a self-knowledge of deception. It has been argued that all humans without exception are highly susceptible to self-deception, since everyone has an emotional baggage of beliefs that can be irrational. Some evolutionary biologists suggest that deception is an important part of human behavior, the instinct for self-deception may have given human agencies a selective advantage: if someone believes their own lie (for example their own presentation biased towards their own interests)), will be better or better able to persuade others of

their "truth".